ABC Programmer's Handbook

ABC Programmer's Handbook

Leo Geurts, Lambert Meertens and Steven Pemberton

CWIU (Centre for Mathematics and Computer Science)
Amsterdam

Prentice Hall
New York   London   Toronto   Sydney   Tokyo   Singapore

First published 1990 by
Prentice Hall International (UK) Ltd
66 Wood Lane End, Hemel Hempstead
Hertfordshire HP2 4RG
A division of
Simon & Schuster International Group

© Prentice Hall International (UK) Ltd, 1990

All rights reserved. No part of this publication may be
reproduced, stored in a retrieval system, or transmitted,
in any form, or by any means, electronic, mechanical,
photocopying, recording or otherwise, without prior
permission, in writing, from the publisher.
For permission within the United States of America
contact Prentice Hall Inc., Englewood Cliffs, NJ 07632.

Printed and bound in Great Britain at the
University Press, Cambridge

ISBN 0-13-000027-2

Library of Congress Cataloging-in-Publication Data
British Library Cataloguing in Publication Data
are available from the publisher.

1 2 3 4 5   94 93 92 91 90

Contents

Preface ix

1 A Quick Look at ABC 1
  1.1 An Example 1
  1.2 Types 2
      1.2.1 Numbers 2
      1.2.2 Texts 3
      1.2.3 Compounds 4
      1.2.4 Lists 4
      1.2.5 Tables 6
      1.2.6 Generic operations 7
  1.3 User-defined Commands and Functions 7
  1.4 Names and Locations 9
  1.5 Control Commands 10
  1.6 Random 11
  1.7 Tests 11
  1.8 Input/Output 13
  1.9 Refinements 13

2 Examples of ABC 15
  2.1 Introduction 15
  2.2 Two First Examples 15
      2.2.1 A telephone list 15
      2.2.2 A guessing game 21
  2.3 Some Common Data-structures 23
      2.3.1 Stacks 23
      2.3.2 Sequences 24
      2.3.3 Sets 28
      2.3.4 Queues 29
      2.3.5 Trees 31
      2.3.6 Graphs 33
  2.4 Numbers 37
      2.4.1 Primes 37
      2.4.2 Recurring fractions 38
      2.4.3 Pi 41
      2.4.4 Polynomials 41

Contents

- 2.5 Sense and Sentence 46
  - 2.5.1 An oracle 46
  - 2.5.2 Eliza 46
  - 2.5.3 A simple document formatter 49
  - 2.5.4 A cross-referencer 52
  - 2.5.5 Imitation 55
  - 2.5.6 Generating sentences 57

3 Using ABC 63
- 3.1 Introduction 63
- 3.2 Typing to ABC 63
  - 3.2.1 Suggestions 64
  - 3.2.2 Undoing mistakes 64
  - 3.2.3 Typing brackets and quotes 65
- 3.3 Immediate Commands 66
  - 3.3.1 Permanent locations 67
  - 3.3.2 Deleting locations 67
  - 3.3.3 Finishing an ABC session 67
  - 3.3.4 Other immediate commands 68
  - 3.3.5 Interrupting a running command 68
- 3.4 More on Typing 69
  - 3.4.1 Indentation 69
  - 3.4.2 Capital letters 70
  - 3.4.3 Redisplaying the screen 70
- 3.5 The Focus 71
  - 3.5.1 Moving the focus up and down lines 71
  - 3.5.2 Correcting whole lines 71
- 3.6 Making your own Commands 72
  - 3.6.1 Functions 73
  - 3.6.2 Predicates 74
  - 3.6.3 Refinements 75
  - 3.6.4 Making changes 76
  - 3.6.5 Correcting errors 77
  - 3.6.6 Renaming and deleting how-to's 78
- 3.7 Other Focus Moves 78
  - 3.7.1 Making the focus smaller 79
  - 3.7.2 Making the focus larger 80
  - 3.7.3 Moving the focus sideways 82
  - 3.7.4 Moving a single hole 84
  - 3.7.5 Using a mouse 84
- 3.8 Copying and Recording 85
  - 3.8.1 Dealing with brackets and quotes 87
  - 3.8.2 Recording 87

3.9 Workspaces 88
    3.9.1 Changing the contents of locations 89
    3.9.2 Moving things between workspaces 89
3.10 Some Common Mistakes 90
    3.10.1 Uninitialised locations 90
    3.10.2 Incompatible types 90
    3.10.3 Ambiguous expressions 91
3.11 An Example 92
3.12 Summary of Operations 95
    3.12.1 Running ABC non-interactively 96

4 Description of ABC 97

4.1 General Issues 97
    4.1.1 Values in ABC 97
    4.1.2 Syntax description method 99
    4.1.3 Representations 101
4.2 How-to's 103
    4.2.1 Command how-to's 103
    4.2.2 Function how-to's 104
    4.2.3 Predicate how-to's 105
    4.2.4 Refinements 106
4.3 Commands 108
    4.3.1 SHARE 109
    4.3.2 CHECK 110
    4.3.3 PUT 110
    4.3.4 WRITE 111
    4.3.5 READ 112
    4.3.6 SET RANDOM 113
    4.3.7 REMOVE 113
    4.3.8 INSERT 113
    4.3.9 DELETE 114
    4.3.10 PASS 114
    4.3.11 QUIT 115
    4.3.12 RETURN 115
    4.3.13 REPORT 116
    4.3.14 SUCCEED 116
    4.3.15 FAIL 117
    4.3.16 User-defined commands 117
    4.3.17 Refined commands 119
    4.3.18 IF 119
    4.3.19 SELECT 120
    4.3.20 WHILE 121
    4.3.21 FOR 121

4.4 Expressions 122
    4.4.1 Numerals 124
    4.4.2 Address inspections 125
    4.4.3 Table selections 125
    4.4.4 Train displays 126
    4.4.5 Formulas 128
    4.4.6 Refined expressions 135
4.5 Addresses 136
    4.5.1 Text-selection addresses 138
    4.5.2 Table-selection addresses 139
4.6 Tests 139
    4.6.1 Order tests 140
    4.6.2 Examinations 141
    4.6.3 Refined tests 142
    4.6.4 Conjunctions 143
    4.6.5 Disjunctions 143
    4.6.6 Negations 144
    4.6.7 Quantifications 144

A ABC Quick Reference 147

B Differences between ABC and B 151

C ABC Implementations 153

Index 159

Preface

WHY ABC?

The answer to the question 'Why a new language?' is the same as the answer to the question 'Why new computers?': because they can help you do the job better. With the choice between a language where it will take a week to write a program, and a language where it will take an afternoon, most people will choose the latter.

ABC is a powerful, easy-to-learn and easy-to-use interactive programming language, intended for personal computing and designed as a modern alternative to BASIC and an easy alternative to Pascal. It supports data structuring and structured programming. As it turns out, ABC is even easier to learn and use than BASIC, and a more powerful tool than Pascal.

ABC is not simply a language, it is a language embedded in a dedicated system. Programming in ABC has a strongly interactive feel. Rather than writing one long program, one develops a set of commands, functions and data that are kept by the system until they are intentionally deleted.

ABC is the result of several years' research towards a language that is simple to learn but easy to use. It was started in 1975 as an attempt to produce a reasonable replacement for BASIC, with as initial aims that it should be

- simple
- interactive
- structured.

ABC is the fourth iteration in this development and reflects several important ideas:

- that 'simple to use' is not the same as 'simple to implement': compare automatic transmission with manual gears in cars;
- that ever more powerful computers mean that programming languages no longer have to squeeze the last drop of power from the processor: programmer time has become more important than computer time.

We started off designing a language for beginners, but the resulting language has become a pleasure to use for both beginners and 'experts' alike.

APPLICATION AREA

ABC doesn't offer any new programming 'paradigm' or method of programming: it is an algorithmic language (like BASIC, Pascal, C or Forth), intended for personal computing. You use it for the sort of programming that BASIC, Pascal or Forth would normally be used for: general everyday programming. ABC is not a systems-programming language, though it is an excellent vehicle for expressing and developing systems-programming type algorithms.

MAJOR POINTS

The advantages of ABC can only really be appreciated by looking at example programs, or better still by writing them. In fact, simply listing the features of the language is just as likely to elicit the response 'so what?'. However, the following are a number of the principal properties of ABC.

Simple

ABC is very simple to learn. For example, whereas Pascal has 13 data types, and C has 19, ABC has only 5. However, this simplicity is not at the expense of expressibility: the data types have been chosen very carefully to allow data structures like sets, trees, dictionaries, and so on, to be easily defined.

ABC is also simple to use. Because of the high-level tools supplied in the language, powerful programs are easy to write and manage.

Compact

ABC programs are typically 4 or 5 times shorter than the equivalent Pascal or C program. However, this is not at the expense of readability by using unfamiliar hieroglyphics. In fact, the shortness makes programs clearer.

ABC can be likened to the 'pseudo-code' that is used when designing a program, except that ABC code is executable.

Structured

ABC has the usual flow of control commands, like IF, WHILE and so on, means for defining your own commands and functions, and even a way of expressing program refinements, to support top-down programming (there is no GO TO). Data structures are also structured.

Expressive

ABC is problem oriented, so you can express your problems at the level that you conceive them. It also allows you to create your own data structures, commands and functions, and so extend the language to your own needs. This can be likened to the way you define 'words' in Forth, but then in a readable way.

Unified

Many concepts in other languages have been unified in ABC. For instance, the division between 'variables' and 'files' in other languages reflects that computers have a two-level store: main store and disk. In a traditional language, if you want to save a data structure between runs of a program, you have to explicitly convert the data structure to textual form and write it to a file, and read it back and reconstruct the structure the next time. ABC doesn't distinguish between levels of store. Global locations (variables) are kept between sessions, so you don't have to explicitly save them yourself. This approach has the advantage that the language is kept small — there is no need for special file-handling commands — and it gives the user much more power, since the operations available on datatypes are at a much higher level than the file-handling facilities in most other languages.

Other languages distinguish between (built-in) commands (or statements) of the language, user-defined procedures, and programs. ABC just has commands. Some are built in, the user can define new ones, and a command is just the same as a program. This of course also simplifies passing parameters to a program: if it is possible at all in other languages, it is usually done using a completely different mechanism than that for passing parameters to a procedure. Since ABC doesn't distinguish between program and command, you use the same mechanism for both.

High-level

Traditional programming languages supply low-level facilities that can be used to build high-level tools. ABC works the other way round: you get high-level tools that you can also use for low-level purposes. For example:

- Sorting is automatic and the default in ABC. Usually that is either what you want or it makes no difference to your program either way. But if you don't want sorting, it is no extra work.
- Pointers are used in other languages to build higher-level data structures. Often these data structures (like trees) are used for sorting and searching purposes, which you get automatically in ABC. But if you really do need a pointer-like facility, you can make one, but with additional benefits, such as being able to print the data structure out.
- Numbers in traditional languages are usually limited in size and accuracy. If you want multi-length or extended precision, you must write a package yourself using the supplied facilities. In ABC, numbers in general are unbounded in length and accuracy.

— Arrays are traditionally non-sparse. If you want sparse arrays, you have to write a package yourself. In ABC you use 'tables' sparsely or non-sparsely with no difference in effort.

Obvious

The language has been designed to be unsurprising for the new programmer. For instance, there are no size limits built into the language. Numbers may be as long as you want, as may texts (strings), all this without having to give a maximum size in advance.

The behaviour of the language is consistent. You may return any value, and any type of value, from a function. You may store any type of value in a location. A program may write out any type of value.

Interactive

Any command you type at the terminal gets executed immediately. All values are visible: you can always write them out to see what's in them.

Even though there are no declarations, there is type checking, by ensuring that locations are used consistently. This gives you the added security that declarations would normally give you, without you having to provide them.

Ease of typing is given not by using very short keywords, but through the system giving suggestions and command completion. Indentation is used to group commands, so no BEGIN-END structure is necessary.

ABC is a programming language and environment. This environment shows one face to the user: the command language is ABC, so you don't have to learn another language in order to manage the system. The system knows about the structure of ABC and so supplies suggestions, indentation, matching brackets and so on automatically. You are always in the editor, so you can edit immediate commands and program input in exactly the same way that you edit commands and functions.

EXPERIENCE

As mentioned before, ABC is the result of several years' development, so that we have had ample time to evaluate and tune the language.

The language is now in use in schools, universities, research institutes and companies around the world, and we are extremely satisfied with and enthusiastic about the results. Many people use ABC as their primary programming language.

The implementation of ABC is an interpreter, which means of course that programs run slower than the equivalent program written in a compiled language. On the other hand, it takes much less time to write a program, which must be taken into account. But even if a given program must run as fast as possible, ABC is still a good choice for developing the algorithms for the program, and prototyping the program.

ABOUT THIS BOOK

This book is an introduction to ABC and its implementations, for people who have already programmed.

It consists of first a quick introduction, giving a brief and informal overview of the whole language. This is followed by a chapter of example programs. These examples demonstrate ABC style, and how you program some common data structures in the language. After that is a user's guide to using the ABC implementations, explaining how to use the ABC system, how to manage ABC programs, and so on. Finally, there is the Description of ABC, a semi-formal definition of the language, giving the syntax and semantics of the language, and the definition of the built-in commands and functions.

If you are sitting at a computer terminal or PC reading this and trying ABC at the same time, you should read the chapter on using ABC first.

There are two things that this book isn't. Firstly, a beginner's introduction to programming in general: a beginner has completely different needs than can be supplied in a book like this. Secondly, it isn't a justification or rationale of why ABC is like it is. There are so many reasons for each detail of ABC, that this book would be swamped with detail. Both of these are separate books currently in preparation.

IMPLEMENTATIONS

The current implementations are for Unix machines, the IBM PC or compatibles, the Apple Macintosh, and the Atari ST. For all these versions you need at least 512k bytes of memory.

The implementations are available on many bulletin-boards and servers. For the Unix version you get the sources to the system, for the other versions you get a binary. They are not 'public-domain': they are copyrighted, but free. This means that you may give them to, or get them from, your friends. So first try to get it from a friend, user-group, or server.

If you don't succeed, the implementations are also available at cost from the authors, so write to us. Share the cost with some friends. There is an order form at the end of the book.

If you do get a copy from someone else, register with us to let us know. In that way you can learn what the latest version is, and make sure you're up to date. It only costs you a stamp.

The address to write to is:

ABC Implementations
CWI/AA
Postbox 4079
1009 AB Amsterdam
The Netherlands

You may also contact us by electronic mail on the UUCP network, or any network that has a connection to it. The address is:

    abc@cwi.nl

There is also an ABC newsletter, published by us at irregular intervals, with example programs, discussions of techniques, and news about new publications and other developments. This is also obtainable from the above address.

ACKNOWLEDGEMENTS

Many people have been involved over the years with our group and the development of the language. Principally should be mentioned Frank van Dijk, Timo Krijnen and Guido van Rossum, who have written large parts of the implementations, and put a lot of personal effort into making ABC what it is, and Eddy Boeve, who though he joined the project at a late stage, was responsible for much of the Atari ST implementation.

CHAPTER 1

A Quick Look at ABC

1.1 AN EXAMPLE

```
HOW TO PRINT CELSIUS FROM a TO b:
   PUT a, b IN lo, hi
   IF lo > hi:
      PUT hi, lo IN lo, hi   \Swap hi and lo
   FOR f IN {lo..hi}:
      PUT (f-32)*5/9 IN c
      WRITE f, "Fahrenheit =", 2 round c, "Celsius" /
```

Once this piece of ABC (the definition of a command PRINT CELSIUS for listing temperatures in degrees Fahrenheit converted to degrees Celsius) has been entered, you can give this command:

```
PRINT CELSIUS FROM 40 TO 45
```

You then get the following on your screen (we use a slanting font for output from ABC):

40 Fahrenheit = 4.44 Celsius
41 Fahrenheit = 5.00 Celsius
42 Fahrenheit = 5.56 Celsius
43 Fahrenheit = 6.11 Celsius
44 Fahrenheit = 6.67 Celsius
45 Fahrenheit = 7.22 Celsius

The text of this *how-to* is straightforward:

- The top line shows the name of the command, and the *template parameters* a and b, which are in lower case.
- PUT has an *expression* to the left of IN, and an *address* to the right. The expression is evaluated to give a *value*, and the address to give a *location*. The value is then put in the location. As we shall see later, this multiple PUT command in fact puts one *compound* value in one *compound* location. The second PUT command swaps the values of lo and hi.
- A comment begins with a back-slash character '\', and continues to the end of the line. A comment can come after a command, or occur on a line by itself.
- A control command, such as IF or FOR, controls the indented commands following the

corresponding colon. Thus, the user need not bother about pairs of BEGIN and END or other delimiters for grouping commands. For the same reason, the whole body of the how-to has been indented. If there is only one controlled command, the whole construction may be displayed on a single line:

```
IF a < 0: PUT -a IN a
```

- The FOR command traverses the list of numbers which starts at lo and ends with hi.
- The round function in the WRITE command rounds its right operand to 2 digits after the decimal point, as indicated by its left operand.
- The / at the end of the WRITE command specifies transition to a new line.

In the ABC system a friendly editor takes care of the tedious aspects of typing the program, such as indentation and other layout matters, capitals, keywords such as PUT and WRITE, etc. This is explained in chapter 3, Using ABC.

1.2 TYPES

The power of ABC is largely due to its carefully designed system of data types and associated operations. There are two basic types — *numbers* and *texts* — and three structures creating new types from existing ones — *compounds*, *lists* and *tables*.

1.2.1 Numbers

Integers, that is, whole numbers, in ABC are unusual in that there is no restriction on length. Furthermore, integers are just a special case of *exact*, i.e. rational, numbers (integral fractions). For example, 1.25 is an exact number. Calculations on exact numbers with the operators +, -, * (multiplication) and / (division), give exact results.

In addition to exact numbers, there are *approximate* (floating point) numbers. The operator ~ is used for conversion to an approximate number: ~22/7 does not return an exact, but an approximate number. Calculations with the mathematical functions like root, sin, and log, return approximate numbers. The function exactly converts an approximate number to exact.

Mixed arithmetic is allowed, as in 2*sin(x-1).

Operations:	Examples:
plain arithmetic	+x, x+y, -x, x-y, x*y, x/y
to the power	3**2 = 9
round upwards	ceiling 3.68 = 4
round downwards	floor 3.68 = 3
round to nearest integer	round 3.68 = 4

round to n digits after decimal point	`1 round 3.68 = 3.7`
sign	`sign 3.68 = 1`
absolute value	`abs(-3.68) = 3.68`
square root	`root 2 = ~1.4142135623731`
n-th root	`3 root 2 = ~1.2599210498949`
remainder after division	`27 mod 10 = 7`
numerator of exact number	`*/ 1.25 = 5`
denominator of exact number	`/* 1.25 = 4`
natural logarithm	`log 10 = ~2.302585092994`
logarithm to base b	`2 log 8 = ~3`
exponential function	`exp 1 = ~2.718281828459`
trigonometric functions	`sin x, cos x, tan x,`
	`arctan x, angle(x, y)`
trigonometric functions in degrees	`360 sin x, 360 cos x,`
	`360 tan x, 360 arctan x,`
	`360 angle (x, y)`
distance from origin	`radius(x, y)`

The functions `*/` and `/*` yield the numerator and the denominator of an exact number. For this purpose, fractions are automatically reduced to lowest terms; so 1.25 = 125/100 is reduced to 5/4. Again, there is no restriction on the lengths of the numerator and denominator. The following definition for the greatest-common-divisor function of two exact positive numbers uses this property (as long as a and b are not 0):

```
HOW TO RETURN gcd(a, b): RETURN a / */(a/b)
```

1.2.2 Texts

`"Merry Christmas"` is an example of a text. Like numbers, there is no restriction on the length of texts.

Operations:	Examples:
join	`"now"^"here" = "nowhere"`
repeat	`"_"^^5 = "_____"`
tail	`"nowhere"@3 = "where"`
head	`"nowhere"|2 = "no"`
number of characters	`#"nowhere" = 7`
number of occurrences	`"e"#"nowhere" = 2`
selection	`"nowhere" item 4 = "h"`
traverse the characters	`FOR c IN "nowhere":`
	`PUT freq[c]+1 IN freq[c]`
smallest character	`min "nowhere" = "e"`
largest character	`max "nowhere" = "w"`
convert to upper case	`upper "NowHere" = "NOWHERE"`

convert to lower case	lower "NowHere" = "nowhere"
strip spaces	stripped " nowhere " = "nowhere"

For the operations @, |, and item, the elements of a text are numbered from 1 to the length of the text.

The operations @ and | may be combined to yield any subtext; for example, to obtain the subtext starting at position 3 and having length 4, we may write:

```
"nowhere"@3|4 = "wher"
```

Such *text selections* may also be used as addresses. For instance, after

```
PUT "nowhere" IN word
PUT "bless" IN word@3|4
```

the location word contains "noblesse" (since wher has been replaced by bless).

1.2.3 Compounds

A compound is a sequence of values of possibly different types. It is like a record in other languages, but it has no field names. Compounds are useful for multiple PUTs, for parameters, for multi-dimensional tables (t[i, j]), but also as values to be put in a table (instead of separate values put in separate tables under the same key). Examples:

```
PUT a, b, c IN b, c, a \cyclic permutation
PUT "May", 22 IN anniversary
PUT 1813, anniversary IN date
PUT date IN year, (month, day)
```

1.2.4 Lists

A list is a *sorted* sequence of values with multiple occurrences allowed. For example,

```
WRITE {"u"; "e"; "a"; "y"; "o"; "i"}
```

gives *{"a"; "e"; "i"; "o"; "u"; "y"}*,

```
WRITE {3; 2; 1}
```

gives *{1; 2; 3}*, and

```
FOR i IN {"ay"; "i"; "eye"; "aye"}: WRITE #i
```

gives *2 3 3 1* (which is because {"ay"; "i"; "eye"; "aye"} gives {"ay"; "aye"; "eye"; "i"}).

The items of a list may be of any type, but all must be of the same type (all texts, or all numbers, etc.) Since there may be multiple occurrences of an entry, you may have lists like {1; 1; 1}.

Sorted lists of any type work because an order is associated with each type. For instance:

```
2.99 < 3.00
"" < "Z" < "a" < "az" < "b"
("b", "c") < ("z", "a")
{} < {"a"; "z"} < {"b"}
```

Instead of {1; 2; 3; 4; 5; 6; 7} the range notation {1..7} may be used; similarly, {"a".."c"} stands for {"a"; "b"; "c"}. Several of these ranges may be combined: the list {"A".."C"; "a".."c"} contains six items.

Operations:	Examples:
initialise	PUT {"wart"; "eye"; "mouth"} IN face
add item to list	INSERT "nose" IN face
	INSERT "eye" IN face
remove *one* instance	REMOVE "wart" FROM face
number of items	#face = 4
number of occurrences	"eye"#face = 2
traverse the items	FOR f IN face: INSERT f IN f2
smallest (= first) item	min {3; 2} = 2
largest (= last) item	max {3; 2} = 3
selection	{1; 9; 8; 9} item 2 = 8

Because lists are kept sorted there is no need for sorting programs. If a different order is required for the items of a list, it is often useful to create a list of compounds. Suppose texts are wanted in length order:

```
PUT {} IN new.face
FOR feature IN face:
    INSERT #feature, feature IN new.face
```

To output the texts in the desired order, you can then use:

```
FOR length, feature IN new.face: WRITE feature /
```

(note the use of a multiple name following FOR) which would produce:

eye
eye
nose
mouth

1.2.5 Tables

Tables are like arrays or tables in other languages, but the keys (= indices) may be of any type, and need not be consecutive:

```
PUT {} IN price
PUT 3.50 IN price["jam"]
PUT 1.95 IN price["bread"]
PUT 2.45 IN price["butter"]
WRITE price
```

gives as output on the screen:

{["bread"]: 1.95; ["butter"]: 2.45; ["jam"]: 3.50}

Notice that the entries are sorted on the keys. All keys of a table must have the same type, but just as with lists, may be of any type. The items (the stored values) must also all have the same type, but, of course, the types of the keys and the items need not be the same.

Operations:	Examples:
initialise	`PUT {} IN count`
add entries	`FOR f IN face: PUT 0 IN count[f]`
modify entries	`FOR f IN face:`
	`    PUT count[f]+1 IN count[f]`
the list of keys	`keys count = {"eye"; "mouth"; "nose"}`
length	`#count = 3`
number of occurrences	
in the items	`2#count = 1`
number of occurrences	
in the keys	`"nose" # keys count = 1`
traverse the items	`FOR i IN count: PUT s+i IN s`
traverse the keys	`FOR f IN keys count:`
	`    WRITE f, count[f] /`
smallest item	`min count = 1`
smallest key	`min keys count = "eye"`
largest item	`max count = 2`
largest key	`max keys count = "nose"`
selection of an item	`count item 2 = 1`
selection of a key	`keys count item 2 = "mouth"`
delete entry	`DELETE count["nose"]`

The `keys` function plays an important role in nearly all applications of tables.

There is one function on texts, `split`, that splits a text into its space-separated words and returns these as a table:

```
split "  now   here  " = {[1]: "now"; [2]: "here"}
```

1.2.6 Generic operations

As you may have noticed, several of the operations mentioned work equally for texts, lists and tables. Texts, lists and tables together are called *trains*. The generic operations are:

```
#   - the length
min - the smallest item
max - the largest item
item - selection of an item.
```

The `FOR` command also works generically on trains.

When a generic operation is applied to a table, it is the items of the table that are handled, and not the keys, so `min t`, where `t` is a table, gives the smallest *item*, and `min keys t` gives the smallest key.

For `min` and `max` there are also versions with two operands: `i min t` gives the smallest item of `t` that is larger than `i`. Similarly, `i max t` gives the largest item of `t` smaller than `i`. For instance,

```
"i" min {"a"; "e"; "i"; "o"; "u"; "y"} = "o"
"i" max {"a"; "e"; "i"; "o"; "u"; "y"} = "e"
```

1.3 USER-DEFINED COMMANDS AND FUNCTIONS

As shown in the `PRINT CELSIUS` example, new commands may be defined with how-to's:

```
HOW TO APPEND tail TO text: PUT text^tail IN text

HOW TO PREPEND head TO text: PUT head^text IN text

HOW TO PRINT text VERTICALLY:
   FOR c IN text: WRITE c /

HOW TO REVERSE text:
   PUT "" IN reverse
   FOR c IN text: PREPEND c TO reverse
   PUT reverse IN text
```

Once these have been given, the commands

```
PUT "here" IN word
PREPEND "now" TO word
REVERSE word
```

make `word` equal to `"erehwon"`. If we now say

REVERSE word@4|2

word is made equal to "erewhon".

So a command how-to is to ABC what a procedure or sub-routine is to other languages. The general appearance of user-defined commands is the same as that of predefined commands such as PUT ... IN ... (though no control commands of the type WHILE ... : can be defined by the user).

Similarly, users may define their own functions, such as this one which returns the set of different items occurring in a given list:

```
HOW TO RETURN elements collection:
    PUT {} IN unique
    FOR element IN collection:
        IF element not.in unique:    bottom p. 11
            INSERT element IN unique
    RETURN unique
```

The name of the function (elements) and its template operand (collection) occur in the first line (values passed to functions are called *operands*, and those passed to commands are called *parameters*). The how-to should contain one or more RETURN commands, specifying the result, which may be of any type, just as the operand may be.

As well as functions with one operand, you may also define functions with two operands, and functions without operands. Here is a function called with that has two operands list1 and list2, and a function origin that has no operands:

```
HOW TO RETURN list1 with list2:    infix
    FOR i IN list1: INSERT i IN list2
    RETURN list2

HOW TO RETURN origin: RETURN (0, 0, 0)
```

Functions with more than two operands have to be written as functions with one or two compound operands, e.g.,

```
HOW TO RETURN (x, y, z) rotated (pitch, roll, yaw):
```

The function with above appears to change the value of its operand, but such a change does not affect any location outside the how-to: it changes a *copy* of the operand which is thrown away upon termination of the invocation of the function.

In contrast to functions, the execution of a *command* defined by a HOW TO does change the environment when something is PUT IN a parameter; in fact, that is the very purpose of commands. When a operand is given to a function, only its value is passed, whereas in the case of a command, the value of the parameter is passed if it has one, and then after the execution of the command, if the value has been changed it is passed back.

The operands for functions and the parameters for commands require no parentheses (except to indicate priorities). For instance, you can write sin x and

2*sin x. However, you cannot write `sin x * 2` since it is ambiguous, and the system will tell you so. You must write either `(sin x) * 2` or `sin(x*2)`, depending on which you mean. Values of any type may be passed to a how-to, as long as they match up with the operations used in the how-to. For instance, the `elements` function above will work on any train as operand:

```
WRITE elements "Mississippi"
```

gives as output

```
{"M"; "i"; "p"; "s"}
```

1.4 NAMES AND LOCATIONS

If we use a command such as

```
PUT {2; 3; 5; 7} IN primes
```

as an immediate command (as opposed to inside a how-to), a location is created — unless one already exists — whose name is `primes`. The location stays in existence until the command `DELETE primes` is given, and so is referred to as a *permanent* location. Names of locations used inside a how-to are private to that how-to, and the corresponding locations are temporary: they are alive only as long as the invocation of the how-to lasts.

One way of importing permanent locations into a how-to is by using parameters, but there is also another way. If, in the example of the previous section, there is only a single text for APPEND, REVERSE, etc., to work on, it is a nuisance to have to pass it as a parameter each time. The how-to's may then be changed to:

```
HOW TO APPEND tail:
   SHARE text
   PUT text^tail IN text

HOW TO PRINT VERTICALLY:
   SHARE text
   FOR c IN text: WRITE c /
```
etc.

`SHARE text` indicates that the name `text` in this how-to will not use a location private to the how-to, but will refer to a shared permanent location, either already in existence, or to be created during the invocation of the how-to. Other how-to's wishing to refer to the same `text` should now also `SHARE text`, since otherwise their use of the name `text` would be private and would introduce a temporary location.

A location should be used consistently for values of one type. Private names may be used for different types of values during the execution of different invocations, but during one invocation the corresponding location may contain only values of the same type. So, if we have defined this SWAP command:

```
HOW TO SWAP a AND b: PUT a, b IN b, a
```

we may use it at one time to swap two numbers, at another time to swap two texts, but never to swap a number and a text.

The system checks this partly statically, i.e. at the time the how-to's are typed in, partly dynamically, i.e. during execution time. Checking is done on a basis of consistency, not on a basis of conformity to declarations, which do not exist in ABC.

1.5 CONTROL COMMANDS

There are two conditional commands. In addition to

```
IF test: ...
```

(no ELSE allowed), ABC also has

```
SELECT:
    test1: ...
    test2: ...
    test3: ...
```

The first test to succeed determines which alternative is to be executed. At least one test must succeed. Instead of the last test, the keyword ELSE may be used, which always succeeds:

```
SELECT:
    e > 0: INSERT e IN pos
    e < 0: INSERT e IN neg
    ELSE: PUT nzero+1 IN nzero
```

For repetition, apart from FOR ... IN ..., there is also

```
WHILE test: ...
```

to repeatedly execute a group of commands while the test is true.

For leaving a command how-to before its end, the command

```
QUIT
```

is used. It may occur anywhere inside a command how-to.

1.6 RANDOM

The function random returns an arbitrary approximate number, such that 0 <= random < 1.

The function choice returns an arbitrary item from a train. For instance, the command

    PUT choice {"A".."Z"} IN cap

puts an arbitrary capital letter in cap. Likewise,

    PUT choice "Mississippi" IN c

puts an arbitrary letter from the text "Mississippi" in c. In the same way, it is possible to make an arbitrary choice from the items of a table. The meaning of choice may be described in terms of random in the following way:

    HOW TO RETURN choice train:
        RETURN train item (1+floor(random*#train))

(This is another example of a how-to which may be used with operands of different types — text, list or table in this case — as long as they are consistent with the operations inside.)

The behaviour of choice and random is based on a pseudo-random sequence. To make programs replicable, the sequence may be started at a specified point by using a SET RANDOM command, e.g. like this:

    SET RANDOM "Today is my birthday."

or with an invocation with any other expression of any type as a parameter.

1.7 TESTS

An order is associated with each type, so <, <=, =, >=, > and <> (unequal) are defined for all values having the same type (but not for values of different types). Multiple comparisons are allowed:

    WHILE x < y < z: PUT f y IN y

To discover if a list or table (or text) contains a certain item (or character), the in test may be used:

    SELECT:
        i in keys count: PUT count[i]+1 IN count[i]
        ELSE: PUT 1 IN count[i]

Similarly, the test not.in tests the absence of an item.

To discover if a number is exact or approximate, the test `exact` is used:

```
SELECT:
    exact x: WRITE */ x, "over", /* x
    ELSE: WRITE "~", x
```

Tests may be combined with AND, OR and NOT:

```
IF i in keys t AND t[i] > 2: ...
IF NOT (c = "a" OR c = "b"): ...
```

Such combined tests are performed from left to right. In an AND combination, evaluation stops as soon as a failing test is encountered; in an OR combination it stops at the first succeeding test.

ABC also has versions of the mathematical quantifiers SOME, EACH and NO:

```
IF SOME d IN {2..n-1} HAS n mod d = 0:
    WRITE n, "has factor", d
```

If the SOME test succeeds, the first value found to satisfy the test following HAS is put in the location of the name between SOME and IN. Examples of NO and EACH are:

```
IF NO year, anniversary IN birthday HAS year = 1813:
    WRITE "list is incomplete"
```

```
SELECT:
    EACH name IN keys birthday HAS name|1 in "ABC":
        WRITE "ABC-composers abound"
    ELSE: WRITE name
```

Just as a new function may be defined with HOW TO RETURN, a new predicate to be used in tests may be defined with HOW TO REPORT:

```
HOW TO REPORT a includes b:
    REPORT EACH x IN b HAS x in a
```

In a predicate how-to, REPORT is used instead of RETURN to indicate the outcome. To avoid REPORT 1 = 1 or REPORT 0 = 1, the commands SUCCEED and FAIL are available as well. Another version of the `includes` how-to might be:

```
HOW TO REPORT a includes b:
    FOR x IN b:
        IF x not.in a: FAIL
    SUCCEED
```

As with HOW TO RETURN, operands are passed by value and the environment is not affected by changes made by a predicate how-to.

1.8 INPUT/OUTPUT

Input from the user at the keyboard is read by a READ command, such as

```
READ size EG (0, 0)
```

where the expression following EG specifies the type of the expression to be entered (here a compound of two numbers). The type of the expected expression may be given by, for example, 0 or "", or by any other expression. In the following example, the READ command demands the input to be of the same type as the items of the list legal.moves:

```
READ move EG min legal.moves
```

READ prompts the user, who may then enter any expression of the desired type, using shared names and built-in or user-defined functions.

READ with an EG format requires input texts to be quoted, just as in ABC itself. For situations where this is a nuisance, another version of the READ command is available:

```
READ line RAW
```

which interprets the input line as a text and stores it in the location line.

For output to the screen, a WRITE command is used. As shown above, WRITE can handle expressions of any type. Apart from the operations mentioned in 1.2.2, the following operations are useful for formatting purposes:

Operation:	Examples:
align left	7*8<<9 = "56 "
align right	7*8>>9 = " 56"
centre	7*8><9 = " 56 "
insert value of expression	"1K is `2**10`" = "1K is 1024"

These operations work for values of any type, and aren't confined to WRITE commands; for instance:

```
PUT "1K is `2**10`" IN message
```

1.9 REFINEMENTS

Hierarchical programming in ABC is aided by refinements. These are like light-weight procedures, but:

- refinements belong to a how-to and are written at its end;
- refinements have no parameters or operands;
- refinements have no private names: the meaning of a name used in a refinement is determined by the context at the point where the refinement is used.

Refinements come in three kinds, analogous to the three kinds of how-to's. All three kinds are seen in this how-to to compute the average of a sequence of positive numbers. Note that just as with commands, functions and predicates, the name of a command-refinement is in capital letters, and the names of function- and predicate-refinements are in lower-case:

```
HOW TO AVERAGE:
   INITIALISE
   GET INPUT
   WHILE valid:
      TREAT
      GET INPUT
   OUTPUT
INITIALISE: PUT 0, 0 IN sum, n
GET INPUT:
   WRITE "Number: "
   READ i EG 0
TREAT: PUT sum+i, n+1 IN sum, n
valid: REPORT i > 0
OUTPUT: WRITE "The average is:", average
average: RETURN sum/n
```

Note that function refinements contain a RETURN command, and predicate refinements a REPORT command. Similarly, command refinements may be left early with the QUIT command. For instance, here is a way of writing the elements of a train until an element is greater than 100:

```
LOOP:
   FOR x IN train:
      IF x > 100: QUIT
      WRITE x
```

Of course, refinements become more useful as programs become longer, and you will see many in the coming chapters.

CHAPTER 2

Examples of ABC

2.1 INTRODUCTION

This chapter gives a number of examples of ABC commands and programs. It is through examples that the advantages of ABC become really clear: that ABC programs are concise, clear and understandable.

The examples in this chapter have been written for clarity, rather than, for instance, efficiency. This reflects one of the aims of ABC, namely to reduce programming time and let the computer do the work. Shorter, clearer programs are easier to program, easier to get right, and easier to change.

The examples often build on previous examples. In particular, the commands and functions from the section on common data-structures are used a lot by later examples.

Several versions of some examples are given in order to demonstrate different programming styles, or to show the effect that different choices of data-structures have.

2.2 TWO FIRST EXAMPLES

To start with we shall give a couple of simple examples. The first, although simple in ABC, would actually demand a lot of programming in another language. It is an especially useful first example since it uses all 5 ABC types.

2.2.1 A telephone list

To maintain a telephone list, you can use an ABC table such as:

    {["Ann"]: 9768; ["Mary"]: 6458}

To create this table, you start off with an empty table, and add the numbers to it (>>> is the prompt for an immediate command):

```
>>> PUT {} IN phone
>>> PUT 6458 IN phone["Mary"]
>>> PUT 9768 IN phone["Ann"]
```

16   *Examples of ABC*

or, in one command:

```
>>> PUT {["Mary"]: 6458; ["Ann"]: 9768} IN phone
```

Looking up someone's number, or changing it, or adding someone else to the list is easy:

```
>>> WRITE phone["Mary"]
6458
>>> PUT 7754 IN phone["John"]
>>> PUT 6348 IN phone["Ann"]
```

You may even write the whole list:

```
>>> WRITE phone
{["Ann"]: 6348; ["John"]: 7754; ["Mary"]: 6458}
```

Note that the entries are printed in alphabetic order. For starting the list, it can be more convenient to have a piece of program to help:

```
HOW TO ADD TO t:
   READ NAME
   WHILE name > "":
      WRITE "Number: "
      READ t[name] EG 0
      READ NAME
READ NAME:
   WRITE "Name: "
   READ name RAW
```

Using this command, you can fill a table `tel` by just typing the names and the numbers:

```
>>> PUT {} IN tel
>>> ADD TO tel
Name: John
Number: 7754
Name: Mary
Number: 6458
Name: Ann
Number: 6348
Name:
>>>
```

To find out who is in the list, you can use the function `keys`:

```
>>> WRITE keys tel
{"Ann"; "John"; "Mary"}
```

If you want to know if there is somebody in `tel` with, say, the number 6348, you can use a so-called *quantifier*:

```
>>> IF SOME name IN keys tel HAS tel[name] = 6348:
        WRITE name
```
Ann

If this happens very often, it may be useful to construct the inverse table, in which you can directly look up the name belonging to a telephone number. Assuming there are no people sharing the same number, the inverse table user can be built this way:

```
>>> PUT {} IN user
>>> FOR name IN keys tel:
        PUT name IN user[tel[name]]
```

and then

```
>>> WRITE user[6348]
```
Ann

though it would be more useful to make these commands into a function to calculate the inverse table:

```
HOW TO RETURN inverse t:
    PUT {} IN inv
    FOR name IN keys t:
        PUT name IN inv[t[name]]
    RETURN inv
```

and then use it like this:

```
>>> PUT inverse tel IN user
>>> WRITE user
```
{[6348]: "Ann"; [6458]: "Mary"; [7754]: "John"}

For printing the table in a neat way you can define this command PRINT TEL:

```
HOW TO PRINT TEL t:
    FOR k IN keys t:
        WRITE k, ":", t[k] /

>>> PRINT TEL tel
```
Ann: 6348
John: 7754
Mary: 6458

The / in the WRITE command writes a newline (note that there is no comma before it). WRITE writes a space between adjacent values, unless they are both texts. So there is a space between the colon and the number, but none between the name and the colon.

To line the columns up, you can use the text operator <<, specifying the width that you want:

18   *Examples of ABC*

```
HOW TO PRINT TEL t:
  FOR k IN keys t:
    WRITE k^":" << 10, t[k] /
```

```
>>> PRINT TEL tel
Ann:      6348
John:     7754
Mary:     6458
```

To print the table as it would be printed in a telephone book, with dots, you can extend the name with a number of dots, and then trim to the width of the column:

```
HOW TO PRINT TEL t:
  FOR k IN keys t:
    WRITE (k ^ "."^^20) | 20, t[k] /
```

```
>>> PRINT TEL tel
Ann.................. 6348
John................. 7754
Mary................. 6458
```

Note that you shouldn't use the expression

```
k^("."^^(20-#k))
```

even though it would appear to mean the same. The difference is that if k is longer than twenty characters, 20-#k is negative, which would cause ^^ to give an error. With the version given, all that would happen is that k would be truncated.

The new command could also be used for the inverse table user, but it makes the assumption that the keys of the table are texts, by using the operator ^ on the keys. In our case, the keys of user are numbers. We can make the command work with any kind of table by converting each key to a text before using it. This works even if the key is already a text. There are two ways to turn a value into a text: by using one of the operators <<, >> or ><, such as k << 1 (the 1 gives the minimum width: it comes out wider if it has to), or by using a conversion, like "`k`".

You'll also notice a space between the dots and the telephone number in the above output from PRINT TEL. This is because, as we said, WRITE writes a space between adjacent values, unless they are both texts. So if we also convert t[k] to a text, we won't get that space:

```
HOW TO PRINT TEL t:
  FOR k IN keys t:
    WRITE ("`k`" ^ "."^^20) | 20, "`t[k]`" /
```

```
>>> PRINT TEL tel
Ann................6348
John...............7754
Mary...............6458

>>> PRINT TEL user
6348...............Ann
6458...............Mary
7754...............John
```

But what if the telephone list *does* contain people who share the same number? In this case, the inverse table will have to be from numbers to *lists* of names. Here is a function that calculates such an inverse table:

```
HOW TO RETURN inverse table:
    PUT {} IN inv
    FOR name IN keys table: ADD NAME
    RETURN inv
ADD NAME:
    IF table[name] not.in keys inv:
        PUT {} IN inv[table[name]]
    INSERT name IN inv[table[name]]
```

The difference with the previous version is contained in the refinement ADD NAME: before, we just stored the name with the number, but now we must store the name in a list. To do this we first have to check that a list has already been started for that number, since you may not insert an item in a non-existent list.

Actually, this sequence is going to occur so often in this chapter, that it is better if we make a separate command of it:

```
HOW TO SAVE item IN table AT key:
    IF key not.in keys table:
        PUT {} IN table[key]
    INSERT item IN table[key]
```

Now inverse looks like this:

```
HOW TO RETURN inverse table:
    PUT {} IN inv
    FOR name IN keys table:
        SAVE name IN inv AT table[name]
    RETURN inv

>>> PUT 6348 IN tel["Sue"]
>>> PUT inverse tel IN users
>>> WRITE users[6348]
{"Ann"; "Sue"}
```

20 *Examples of ABC*

Finally, let us now treat the more realistic case where not only people share telephones, but people may also have more than one telephone. The telephone list must now hold for each name a *list* of numbers. So first we must change ADD TO to accept multiple numbers:

```
HOW TO ADD TO t:
   ASK NAME
   WHILE name > "":
      WRITE "Number: "
      READ no EG 0
      SAVE no IN t AT name
      ASK NAME
ASK NAME:
   WRITE "Name: "
   READ name RAW
```

```
>>> PUT {} IN tel
>>> ADD TO tel
```
Name: John
Number: 7754
Name: Mary
Number: 6458
Name: Mary
Number: 7754
Name: Ann
Number: 6348
Name: Sue
Number: 6348
Name:

```
>>> PRINT TEL tel
```
Ann.................{6348}
John................{7754}
Mary................{6458; 7754}
Sue.................{6348}

Now we must redefine `inverse` so that it can handle the new table. This just involves adding one more line to handle each number for a person rather than just one number:

```
HOW TO RETURN inverse t:
   PUT {} IN inv
   FOR name IN keys t:
      FOR number IN t[name]:
         SAVE name IN inv AT number
   RETURN inv
```

```
>>> PRINT TEL inverse tel
6348...............{"Ann"; "Sue"}
6458...............{"Mary"}
7754...............{"John"; "Mary"}
```

This version of inverse restores a nice property that the very first version had, but that the second didn't: applying inverse twice to a table gives you the original table back:

```
>>> PRINT TEL inverse inverse tel
Ann................{6348}
John...............{7754}
Mary...............{6458; 7754}
Sue................{6348}
```

Of course, telephone numbers are not always pure numbers. They may contain hyphens, brackets, words, or other non-digit characters, like 020-5929333 or WHI-1212x300. To support this, you have to use texts instead of numbers for the telephone numbers. As an exercise, which single line of which how-to in the last part of this section would need to be changed to do this?

2.2.2 A guessing game

Here is a simple guessing game. To make it interesting it uses the function choice, which given any text, list or table will return a random element of it:

```
>>> WRITE choice {1..10}
7
>>> WRITE choice {1..10}
3
>>> WRITE choice {"yes"; "no"; "maybe"}
no

HOW TO GUESS:
   PUT choice {0..99} IN number
   WRITE "Guess my number from 0 to 99: "
   READ guess EG 0
   WHILE guess <> number:
      SELECT:
         guess < number: WRITE "Try higher: "
         guess > number: WRITE "Try lower: "
      READ guess EG 0
   WRITE "Yes! Well done" /
```

Examples of ABC

```
>>> GUESS
Guess my number from 0 to 99: 50
Try lower:  25
Try lower:  15
Try higher: 20
Try lower:  17
Try higher: 19
Yes! Well done
```

Here is the complement game: the computer guesses the number. It works by keeping the list of numbers that the answer must lie in (initially {0..99}). Then as each guess is high or low, the range is restricted accordingly (for instance, if 50 is too low, the list becomes {51..99}). If the list ever becomes empty, the player must have given the wrong answer at some stage.

```
HOW TO PLAY:
    WRITE "Think of a number from 0 to 99,"
    WRITE " and press [return]: "
    READ return RAW
    PUT {0..99} IN range
    WHILE range <> {}: TRY range

HOW TO TRY range:
    PUT choice range IN guess
    WRITE "Is it `guess`? "
    READ reply RAW
    SELECT:
        reply|1 = "y":
            PUT {} IN range
            WRITE "Good" /
        reply|1 = "h": PUT {min range..guess-1} IN range
        reply|1 = "l": PUT {guess+1..max range} IN range
        ELSE: WRITE "Please reply y(es), h(igh) or l(ow)" /
    IF range = {} AND reply|1 <> "y": WRITE "Cheat!" /

>>> PLAY
Think of a number from 0 to 99, and press [return]:
Is it 17? no
Please reply y(es), h(igh) or l(ow)
Is it 33? l
Is it 53? h
Is it 45? l
Is it 50? y
Good
```

```
>>> PLAY
Think of a number from 0 to 99, and press [return]:
Is it 93? l
Is it 96? h
Is it 94? h
Cheat!
```

2.3 SOME COMMON DATA-STRUCTURES

Each programming language has its own style and idioms. People who have used other programming languages sometimes unnecessarily use techniques from those other languages when programming in ABC. For instance, when using a stack, they keep both the stack, and the index of its top element. Here then are a few examples of how you use some of the standard data-structures in ABC.

2.3.1 Stacks

You can represent a stack using a table, with integers as the keys and the elements of the stack as items. You don't need to keep a separate index to the top item because you can always use the ABC # operator to find out the size of the stack.

Emptying or initialising a stack is easy:

```
HOW TO EMPTY stack:
    PUT {} IN stack
```

To add an item you can use the following command:

```
HOW TO PUSH item ON stack:
    PUT item IN stack[#stack+1]
```

Here it is in use:

```
>>> EMPTY numbers
>>> PUSH 123 ON numbers
>>> WRITE numbers
{[1]: 123}
>>> PUSH 321 ON numbers
>>> WRITE numbers
{[1]: 123; [2]: 321}
```

You can access the top item of the stack with the following function:

```
HOW TO RETURN top stack:
    RETURN stack[#stack]
```

and pop the top element with this command:

```
HOW TO POP stack INTO item:
    PUT stack[#stack] IN item
    DELETE stack[#stack]
```

Here is an example using these commands, a command to replace the top two elements of a stack with their sum:

```
HOW TO ADD stack:
    POP stack INTO right
    POP stack INTO left
    PUSH left+right ON stack
```

and then a use of this command:

```
>>> EMPTY numbers
>>> PUSH 123 ON numbers
>>> PUSH 321 ON numbers
>>> ADD numbers
>>> WRITE top numbers
444
```

Note that because functions in ABC cannot have side-effects, you can only use a function to pop a stack by returning both the popped element and the stack:

```
HOW TO RETURN popped stack:
    PUT stack[#stack] IN item
    DELETE stack[#stack]
    RETURN item, stack
```

Using this, ADD would look like this:

```
HOW TO ADD stack:
    PUT popped stack IN right, stack
    PUT popped stack IN left, stack
    PUSH left+right ON stack
```

2.3.2 Sequences

ABC's lists are sorted, and that is often what you need, or at least it makes no difference to your program whether they are sorted or not. However, sometimes you need to store an unsorted sequence of items. The standard way to do this in ABC is to store each item in a table whose keys are ascending integers.

So the empty sequence, just like the empty stack, is an empty table {}. Appending an item to a sequence uses the same idea as for stacks:

```
HOW TO APPEND item TO sequence:
    PUT item IN sequence[#sequence+1]
```

This method of adding items to the end of a sequence only works if items are not re moved, or are removed only from the end. If this is not the case, then you have to use this version:

```
HOW TO APPEND item TO sequence:
    PUT item IN sequence[next]
next:
    SELECT:
        #sequence = 0: RETURN 1
        ELSE: RETURN 1 + max keys sequence
```

As an example, suppose you want to write a HELP command that gives help on various topics. Each help message can be stored as a sequence of lines that can be displayed with this command:

```
HOW TO DISPLAY message:
    FOR line IN message:
        WRITE line /
```

Each message can then be stored in a table with the topics as keys. To add a help message for some new topic, you can use the following command:

```
HOW TO ADD HELP FOR topic:
    SHARE help
    PUT {} IN help[topic]
    WRITE "Type lines of help. "
    WRITE "Finish with a '.' alone on a line." /
    READ line RAW
    WHILE line <> ".":
        APPEND line TO help[topic]
        READ line RAW
```

So that finally, the help command can look like this:

```
HOW TO HELP topic:
    SHARE help
    SELECT:
        topic in keys help: DISPLAY help[topic]
        ELSE: WRITE "Sorry, I can't help with that" /
```

although we could make it a bit more useful for the user by adding the ability to list what topics are available:

```
HOW TO HELP topic:
   SHARE help
   SELECT:
      topic in keys help: DISPLAY help[topic]
      ELSE:
         WRITE "Sorry, I can't help with that. "
         WRITE "These are the topics I know: " /
         LIST keys help
```

This uses the following command to print a list neatly:

```
HOW TO LIST l:
   PUT "" IN separator
   FOR item IN l:
      WRITE separator, item<<1
      PUT ", " IN separator
   WRITE /

>>> LIST {1..5}
1, 2, 3, 4, 5
>>> LIST {"READ"; "WRITE"; "PUT"}
PUT, READ, WRITE
```

This method of writing the separating comma may seem a bit unusual at first, but is preferable to the alternatives, where rather than just traversing the list, you have to index each item separately with `item`, and include a test:

```
HOW TO LIST l:
   FOR i IN {1..#l}:
      WRITE l item i << 1
      IF i <> #l:
         WRITE ", "
   WRITE /
```

or

```
HOW TO LIST l:
   FOR i IN {1..#l-1}:
      WRITE l item i << 1, ", "
   IF #l > 0:
      WRITE l item #l
   WRITE /
```

or

```
HOW TO LIST l:
   IF #l > 0:
      WRITE l item 1
      FOR i IN {2..#l}:
         WRITE ", ", l item i << 1
   WRITE /
```

Don't be misled by false feelings of 'efficiency' here: regardless of the size of the value involved, the cost of a PUT command is always the same, and it is one of the cheapest commands there is in ABC (PASS is cheaper). Similarly, a FOR command over a list is (not surprisingly) about half the cost of a FOR over a range and then indexing.

Where output is involved, it is often better to use a function than a command to format a structure on a single line:

```
HOW TO RETURN listed l:
   PUT "", "" IN separator, result
   FOR item IN l:
      PUT result^separator^(item<<1) IN result
      PUT ", " IN separator
   RETURN result
```

Now it can be mixed with other output in a single write:

```
>>> WRITE listed {1..3}
1, 2, 3
>>> WRITE "(", listed {1..3}, ")"
(1, 2, 3)
```

Many of ABC's standard operators and functions are defined in two versions, a *monadic* one (with one operand) and a *dyadic* one (with two operands), where the monadic version is defined in terms of the dyadic one. This is an obvious candidate for this treatment: the dyadic version can also take the separator:

```
HOW TO RETURN separator listed l:
   PUT "", "" IN sep, result
   FOR item IN l:
      PUT result^sep^(item<<1) IN result
      PUT separator IN sep
   RETURN result
```

and then the monadic version can be defined as:

```
HOW TO RETURN listed l: RETURN ", " listed l
```

These can then be used for all sorts of different purposes (note that they work for tables and texts, as well as lists):

```
>>> WRITE listed phone
6348, 7754, 6458
>>> WRITE listed keys phone
Ann, John, Mary
>>> WRITE "." listed "Divorce"
D.i.v.o.r.c.e
```

2.3.3 Sets

ABC's lists are nearly sets. The difference is that they may contain more than one occurrence of an item (which makes them what are called *bags* or *multisets*). Using lists to represent sets, you can use the following command to add an item to a set:

```
HOW TO INCLUDE element IN set:
    IF element not.in set:
        INSERT element IN set
```

The following functions return the union, intersection and difference of two sets:

```
HOW TO RETURN a with b:
    FOR item IN b:
        INCLUDE item IN a
    RETURN a

>>> WRITE {1..4} with {3..6}
{1; 2; 3; 4; 5; 6}

HOW TO RETURN a common.with b:
    FOR item IN a:
        IF item not.in b:
            REMOVE item FROM a
    RETURN a

>>> WRITE {1..4} common.with {3..6}
{3; 4}

HOW TO RETURN a less b:
    FOR item IN a:
        IF item in b:
            REMOVE item FROM a
    RETURN a

>>> WRITE {1..4} less {3..6}
{1; 2}
```

If you have a list, possibly with duplicated entries, or a table (or even a text), and you want to convert it to a set, you can let `with` do all the work:

```
HOW TO RETURN set t:
    RETURN {} with t

>>> WRITE set "Mississippi"
{"M"; "i"; "p"; "s"}
```

Finally, here is a function to calculate the *power set* of a set, that is, the set of all subsets of a set, though it actually works on any train (i.e, text, list, or table):

```
HOW TO RETURN powerset s:
    PUT {{}} IN pset
    FOR item IN s:
        FOR set IN pset:
            INCLUDE set with {item} IN pset
    RETURN pset

>>> FOR s IN powerset "ABC":
        WRITE s /
{}
{"A"}
{"A"; "B"}
{"A"; "B"; "C"}
{"A"; "C"}
{"B"}
{"B"; "C"}
{"C"}
```

2.3.4 Queues

It is a temptation when coming from another language to use sequences to implement queues, and use a technique such as linear search to insert an item in the queue at the right place. However, since ABC's lists are already sorted, you can use them instead, storing the item along with the value that determines its place in the queue.

For instance, suppose you have a queue of tasks to be performed at given times, where the times are given as the number of seconds since midnight. You can insert an item in the queue like this:

```
INSERT time, task IN queue
```

Selecting the first task to be executed can then be done with the following:

30   *Examples of ABC*

```
HOW TO TAKE thing FROM queue:
    PUT queue item 1 IN thing
    REMOVE thing FROM queue
```

invoked with

```
TAKE time, task FROM queue
```

You can use `min queue` instead of `queue item 1` if you want, since it means the same thing for lists.

Here is an example of the use of these commands, a rather unrealistic simulation of a metro train station. People enter the station at random intervals between 0 and 10 seconds. Trains leave at intervals of 10 minutes (600 seconds). The program prints how many people are on each train as it leaves:

```
HOW TO SIMULATE:
    PUT 0, {} IN time, tasks
    NEW TRAIN
    NEW PERSON
    WHILE tasks <> {}: PROCESS TASK
PROCESS TASK:
    TAKE time, task FROM tasks
    SELECT:
        task = "train":
            WRITE "Time `time`: `people` passengers" /
            PUT 0 IN people
            NEW TRAIN
        task = "person":
            PUT people+1 IN people
            NEW PERSON
NEW TRAIN: INSERT time+600, "train" IN tasks
NEW PERSON: INSERT time+random*10, "person" IN tasks

>>> SIMULATE
Time 600: 117 passengers
Time 1200: 125 passengers
Time 1800: 113 passengers
Time 2400: 120 passengers
*** Interrupted
>>>
```

(Since this command never terminates, it would go on and on producing results. To stop such a command, you have to *interrupt* it, and that is the reason for the last line in the output above. How you interrupt a command is explained in chapter 3, Using ABC.)

2.3.5 Trees

The absence of a pointer type in ABC would seem to suggest that data-structures like trees cannot be created. In fact, thanks to tables, they can, and with certain advantages, not least of which is the ease of printing a table.

A tree can be represented in ABC as a table of nodes. It is relatively unimportant what the keys of such a table are; this example uses numbers. Each node then consists of an indication of what kind of node it is (here we will use texts), and a sequence of numbers. These numbers are the keys of the sub-trees of this node.

To add a node to the tree you use the same technique as with stacks and sequences. In fact, the tree can be seen as a sequence of nodes, where you also use the sequence numbers:

```
HOW TO ADD NODE n TO tree GIVING p:
    PUT #tree, n IN p, tree[#tree]
```

(The use of #tree as the index just has the effect that the first element is stored at key 0, the second at 1, and so on.)

To show the use of tables in this way, here is a small program to convert simple arithmetic expressions into trees, a typical example for pointers. For example, the tree for a*2+b*2 can be represented as the following table, starting from node 6:

```
{ [0]: ("a", {});
  [1]: ("2", {});
  [2]: ("*", {[1]: 0; [2]: 1});
  [3]: ("b", {});
  [4]: ("2", {});
  [5]: ("*", {[1]: 3; [2]: 4});
  [6]: ("+", {[1]: 2; [2]: 5})
}
```

The following can be used to display a returned tree:

```
HOW TO DISPLAY TREE t, n:
    WRITE "Top node is", n /
    FOR i IN keys t:
        WRITE i, ": "
        PUT t[i] IN type, nodes
        WRITE type, " " listed nodes /
```

The text of the expression to be compiled is passed over as parameter, and the resulting tree and the index of its top-most node is returned:

```
HOW TO RETURN compiled expression:
    SHARE tree, line
    PUT {}, expression IN tree, line
    EXPRESSION node
    RETURN tree, node
```

32 *Examples of ABC*

The expression is parsed using what is known as *recursive-descent*: EXPRESSION invokes TERM to parse a sub-expression; next.char returns the first character of the expression and SKIP CHAR trims off the first character from the expression.

```
HOW TO EXPRESSION x:
   SHARE tree
   TERM x
   WHILE next.char in {"+"; "-"}:
      PUT next.char IN op
      SKIP CHAR
      TERM y
      ADD NODE (op, {[1]: x; [2]: y}) TO tree GIVING x

HOW TO RETURN next.char:
   SHARE line
   RETURN line|1

HOW TO SKIP CHAR:
   SHARE line
   PUT line@2 IN line
```

TERM is very similar to EXPRESSION. OPERAND recognises a single letter or digit as operand to a sub-expression.

```
HOW TO TERM x:
   SHARE tree
   OPERAND x
   WHILE next.char in {"*"; "/"}:
      PUT next.char IN op
      SKIP CHAR
      OPERAND y
      ADD NODE (op, {[1]: x; [2]: y}) TO tree GIVING x

HOW TO OPERAND x:
   SHARE tree
   SELECT:
      next.char in {"a".."z"; "0".."9"}:
         ADD NODE (next.char, {}) TO tree GIVING x
      ELSE:
         WRITE "Error at:", next.char /
         PUT -1 IN x
      SKIP CHAR
```

```
>>> DISPLAY TREE compiled "a*2+b*2"
Top node is 6
0 : a
1 : 2
2 : * 0 1
3 : b
4 : 2
5 : * 3 4
6 : + 2 5
```

As an example of traversing such a tree, here is a function to evaluate a parsed expression:

```
HOW TO RETURN value (tree, node):
    SHARE memory
    PUT tree[node] IN type, operands
    SELECT:
        type in keys memory: RETURN memory[type]
        type in {"0".."9"}: RETURN #{"1"..type}
        type = "+": RETURN left+right
        type = "-": RETURN left-right
        type = "*": RETURN left*right
        type = "/": RETURN left/right
        ELSE:
            WRITE "*** `type` has no value" /
            RETURN 0
    left: RETURN value (tree, (operands item 1))
    right: RETURN value (tree, (operands item 2))
```

Note the expression #{"1"..type}. This converts a digit character into its numeric value. For instance, if type = "3", then {"1"..type} is {"1"; "2"; "3"}, whose size is 3. Similarly, {"1".."0"} is {}, whose size is 0.

```
>>> PUT {} IN memory
>>> PUT 3, 4 IN memory["a"], memory["b"]
>>> WRITE value compiled "a*2+b*2"
14
```

2.3.6 Graphs

We mean here the mathematical concept of a graph — also called a relation — and not the plotting of functions. A graph is an extension of a tree, where each node may refer to any other node in the graph.

You can represent a graph using the same idea as with trees. Each node can be a key in a table. The associated item of the table can then be a set of nodes.

As a concrete example, take a group of people, and the information of who can contact whom within that group. For instance, contacts["Doris"] = {"Bessy"; "Kevin"} means that Doris can contact Bessy and Kevin (but not necessarily the other way round). Here is a command to display such a graph:

```
HOW TO SHOW graph:
    FOR node IN keys graph:
        WRITE node, ": ", listed graph[node] /

>>> PUT {} IN contacts
>>> PUT {"Emily"; "Kevin"} IN contacts["Doris"]
>>> PUT {"Emily"} IN contacts["Kevin"]
>>> PUT {"Bessy"} IN contacts["Emily"]
>>> SHOW contacts
Doris: Emily, Kevin
Emily: Bessy
Kevin: Emily
```

Here is a function that returns the sub-graph of all people contactable, directly or indirectly, from a given root person (which is a process sometimes called *garbage-collection*). This is a *mark and sweep* version:

```
HOW TO RETURN graph reachable.from root:
    PUT {root}, {root} IN accessible, to.do
    COLLECT REACHABLES
    ELIMINATE UNREACHABLES
    RETURN graph
COLLECT REACHABLES:
    WHILE to.do > {}:
        PUT to.do item 1 IN node
        REMOVE node FROM to.do
        TREAT NODE
TREAT NODE:
    IF node in keys graph:
        FOR n IN graph[node]:
            IF n not.in accessible:
                INSERT n IN accessible
                INSERT n IN to.do
ELIMINATE UNREACHABLES:
    FOR node IN keys graph:
        IF node not.in accessible:
            DELETE graph[node]
```

Here is a *copy* version. It also takes advantage of the how-to's with, less, and TAKE defined earlier:

```
HOW TO RETURN graph reachable.from root:
   PUT {root}, {} IN to.do, new
   WHILE to.do > {}:
      TAKE node FROM to.do
      TREAT NODE
   RETURN new
TREAT NODE:
   IF node in keys graph:
      PUT graph[node] IN new[node]
      PUT to.do with new.nodes IN to.do
new.nodes: RETURN new[node] less keys new

>>> SHOW contacts reachable.from "Kevin"
Emily: Bessy
Kevin: Emily
```

The product of two graphs is the graph where a is connected to c, if a is connected to b in the first graph, and b is connected to c in the second:

```
HOW TO RETURN g1 prod g2:
   PUT {} IN product
   FOR a IN keys g1:
      FOR b IN g1[a]:
         IF b in keys g2:
            PUT product.a with g2[b] IN product[a]
   RETURN product
product.a:
   IF a in keys product: RETURN product[a]
   RETURN {}
```

For instance, take this graph showing the parents of a group of people:

```
>>> SHOW parents
Anne: John, Margaret
John: Gladys, James
Margaret: Alice, George
Mark: John, Margaret
```

The product of this graph with itself gives the graph of grandparents:

```
>>> SHOW parents prod parents
Anne: Alice, George, Gladys, James
Mark: Alice, George, Gladys, James
```

Actually, the telephone list in the first example of this chapter can be seen as a graph, and furthermore, the function inverse defined there inverts any graph. The inverse of the parents graph is the children graph:

```
>>> SHOW inverse parents
Alice: Margaret
George: Margaret
Gladys: John
James: John
John: Anne, Mark
Margaret: Anne, Mark
```

A useful operation on a graph is to calculate its *closure*. A closure of a graph is a graph with the same nodes as the original graph, but where each node refers to all nodes reachable from the node in the original. The closure of the contacts graph, for example, is the graph where each node refers to all contactable nodes, whether directly or indirectly. Here we use the function `with` we defined earlier for sets:

```
HOW TO RETURN closure a:
    FOR i IN keys a:
        FOR j IN keys a:
            IF i in a[j]:
                PUT a[i] with a[j] IN a[j]
    RETURN a
```

To understand how this works, the crucial insight is that after each step of FOR i, the value of the closure graph under construction is such that, for each node j, a[j] is the list of nodes directly or indirectly reachable from j using as contacts only nodes that are at most i.

```
>>> SHOW closure contacts
Doris: Bessy, Emily, Kevin
Emily: Bessy
Kevin: Bessy, Emily
>>> SHOW closure(contacts reachable.from "Kevin")
Emily: Bessy
Kevin: Bessy, Emily
```

The closure of the parents graph shows all the ancestors for each person:

```
>>> SHOW closure parents
Anne: Alice, George, Gladys, James, John, Margaret
John: Gladys, James
Margaret: Alice, George
Mark: Alice, George, Gladys, James, John, Margaret
```

The children of your parents are you and your siblings. So the product of the parents and the children graphs gives the siblings:

```
>>> SHOW parents prod (inverse parents)
Anne: Anne, Mark
John: John
Margaret: Margaret
Mark: Anne, Mark
```

On the other hand, the parents of your children are you and your partner(s), so the product of the children and parents graphs shows who have produced offspring together:

```
>>> SHOW (inverse parents) prod parents
Alice: Alice, George
George: Alice, George
Gladys: Gladys, James
James: Gladys, James
John: John, Margaret
Margaret: John, Margaret
```

2.4 NUMBERS

ABC's numbers have two unusual properties: they are calculated exactly for most operations, and they may have unbounded length.

2.4.1 Primes

Here is a program that uses a list of numbers and the sieve method to calculate primes. It works by taking the set of numbers from 2 to n, then taking the smallest (2). This is a prime. All multiples of this are removed from the list, and then the next smallest (3) is taken, and the same process repeated, and so on.

```
HOW TO SIEVE TO n:
   PUT {2..n} IN set
   WHILE set > {}:
      PUT min set IN p
      REMOVE p FROM s
      WRITE p
      REMOVE MULTIPLES
REMOVE MULTIPLES:
   FOR m IN {p..floor(n/p)}:
      IF m*p in set:
         REMOVE m*p FROM set
```

38   *Examples of ABC*

```
>>> SIEVE TO 50
2 3 5 7 11 13 17 19 23 29 31 37 41 43 47
```

Another way to do this is to use the set functions defined earlier, and make it a function:

```
HOW TO RETURN primes n:
    IF n < 2: RETURN {}
    PUT {2..n} IN set
    FOR p IN primes floor root n:
        PUT set less multiples IN set
    RETURN set
    multiples: RETURN p times {p..floor(n/p)}
```

This uses a function that takes a set of numbers and returns the set with all elements multiplied by a given factor:

```
HOW TO RETURN f times s:
    PUT {} IN res
    FOR i IN s: INSERT f*i IN res
    RETURN res

>>> WRITE 2 times {1..5}
{2; 4; 6; 8; 10}
>>> WRITE primes 45
{2; 3; 5; 7; 11; 13; 17; 19; 23; 29; 31; 37; 41; 43}
```

Notice the use of recursion in the definition of primes:

```
FOR p IN primes floor root 10
```

For instance, to calculate the primes to 1000, it first calculates the primes to 31 (that is, floor root 1000), and removes all multiples of these from the list {2..1000}. While this may seem like a lot of extra work, in fact it results in slightly less work than using

```
FOR p IN {2..floor root n}
```

since the body of the FOR is executed fewer times.

2.4.2 Recurring fractions

The following function can be used to print an exact number out exactly: if it is a fraction, then the fraction is printed either exactly or as a recurring decimal.

It works in the same way that you would do it by hand: by calculating the next digit of the fraction and the remainder then left. With the remainder it saves the position of the digit, so that when the same remainder occurs again, the end of the repeating part has been reached. Then the beginning of the repeated part is the index that was saved with the repeated remainder.

The expression x mod 1 returns the fractional part of x. For instance:

```
>>> WRITE pi mod 1
0.1415926535889793

HOW TO RETURN rep x:
   PUT "`floor x`.", 10*(x mod 1), {} IN t, x, index
   IF x = 0: RETURN t|#t-1 \it was a whole number
   WHILE x not.in keys index:
       PUT #t IN index[x]
       PUT t^"`floor x`", 10*(x mod 1) IN t, x
   RETURN t|index[x] ^ recurring.part
recurring.part:
   IF x = 0: RETURN "" \non-recurring fraction
   RETURN "[" ^ t@index[x]+1 ^ "]"

>>> WRITE rep(22/7)
3.[142857]

>>> FOR i IN {1..15}:
       WRITE i, ": ", rep (1/i) /
1 : 1
2 : 0.5
3 : 0.[3]
4 : 0.25
5 : 0.2
6 : 0.1[6]
7 : 0.[142857]
8 : 0.125
9 : 0.[1]
10 : 0.1
11 : 0.[09]
12 : 0.08[3]
13 : 0.[076923]
14 : 0.0[714285]
15 : 0.0[6]
```

Actually, this function also works for approximate numbers:

```
>>> WRITE rep pi
3.14159265358979322702026593105983920395374298095703125
```

but, by the very nature of approximate numbers, only so many of these digits are accurate. That is to say, the number printed is the closest to the real value of *pi* that could be attained using an approximate number, and this number diverges at some point from the real value of *pi*.

Approximate numbers are the only place where the behaviour of ABC varies between machines, since ABC uses the numeric representation of the machine to represent them, and so you get a different accuracy on different machines. The following command works out what base is used for approximate arithmetic (nowadays that is usually 2, and sometimes 16), and how many digits accuracy in that base are used. It then gives this as the approximate number of decimal digits accuracy.

To understand how it works, imagine that approximate numbers are to base ten, with three digits accuracy. Starting from 2, the command first keeps doubling until it reaches a number that adding 1 to doesn't alter. In our fictitious case, it would try 1, 2, 4, 8, ... 512, and stop at 1024, which is only representable as 1020, since there are only three significant digits, and adding 1 to 1020 still gives 1020.

Then starting at 2 again, it keeps doubling until adding it to the original number gives a different number. For 1020 this is 8 or 16, depending on whether the result of the addition gets rounded up or truncated. In either case the result is 1030. The difference between this and the original number, in our case 1030 − 1020 = 10, is the base.

Once you have that, it is then fairly simple to determine the number of significant digits:

```
HOW TO CALCULATE ACCURACY:
    CALCULATE BASE
    CALCULATE DIGITS
CALCULATE BASE:
    PUT ~2 IN a
    WHILE a+1-a-1 = ~0: PUT a+a IN a
    PUT ~0, ~2 IN base, b
    WHILE base = ~0: PUT a+b-a, b+b IN base, b
    WRITE "Base =", base /
CALCULATE DIGITS:
    PUT 1, base IN sig, b
    WHILE b+1-b-1 = ~0: PUT sig+1, b*base IN sig, b
    WRITE "Significant digits =", sig /
    IF base <> 10:
        WRITE "This is about `decimal` decimal digits" /
decimal: RETURN 1 round ((sig-1)/(base log 10))
```

Here is its output when run on the machine used for this book:

```
>>> CALCULATE ACCURACY
Base = 2
Significant digits = 56
This is about 16.6 decimal digits
```

This means that only the first 16 digits of the above output for pi are useful:

```
>>> WRITE rep (16 round pi)
3.1415926535897932
```

2.4.3 Pi

ABC's unbounded numbers allow you to use the following algorithm to calculate the number *pi* exactly with as many digits as you like. A language with 32 bit integers would only produce the first 5 digits before getting overflow. The ABC program just goes on churning out digits until you interrupt it.

The program works by repeatedly refining a so-called continued fraction that represents *pi*. The first approximation is $\frac{4}{1}$, the second is $\frac{4}{1+\frac{1}{3}}$, which is $\frac{12}{4}$. In the next, the 3 is replaced by $3+\frac{4}{5}$, and in the next after that, the 5 is replaced by $5+\frac{9}{7}$ and so on, so that each part of the fraction is $\frac{k^2}{2k+1+\cdots}$ for $k = 0, 1, 2, \cdots$.

In the program, $\frac{a}{b}$ represents one approximation of the fraction, and $\frac{a'}{b'}$ the next. If there are any leading digits in common, then these are printed, and the next approximation is calculated.

```
HOW TO PI:
    PUT 2, 4, 1, 12, 4 IN k, a, b, a', b'
    WHILE 1=1:
        NEXT APPROXIMATION
        PRINT COMMON DIGITS
NEXT APPROXIMATION:
    PUT k**2, 2*k+1, k+1 IN p, q, k
    PUT a', b', p*a+q*a', p*b+q*b' IN a, b, a', b'
PRINT COMMON DIGITS:
    PUT floor(a/b), floor(a'/b') IN d, d'
    WHILE d = d':
        WRITE d<<1
        PUT 10*(a mod b), 10*(a' mod b') IN a, a'
        PUT floor(a/b), floor(a'/b') IN d, d'

>>> PI
31415926535897932384626433832795028841971693993751058209749445923078 16
*** Interrupted
```

2.4.4 Polynomials

A polynomial is an expression such as $7x^5 - 4x^4 + 3x - 1$ and can be represented in ABC as a table with the powers as keys and the coefficients as items:

  {[5]: 7; [4]: -4; [1]: 3; [0]: -1}

Given this representation, it is then easy to define the sum of two polynomials:

42   *Examples of ABC*

```
HOW TO RETURN a plus b:
    FOR q IN keys b:
        SELECT:
            q in keys a: PUT a[q]+b[q] IN a[q]
            ELSE: PUT b[q] IN a[q]
    RETURN normalised a
```

The function `normalised` removes all zero items:

```
HOW TO RETURN normalised poly:
    FOR k IN keys poly:
        IF poly[k] = 0:
            DELETE poly[k]
    RETURN poly
```

The difference of two polynomials is similar:

```
HOW TO RETURN a minus b:
    FOR q IN keys b:
        SELECT:
            q in keys a: PUT a[q]-b[q] IN a[q]
            ELSE: PUT -b[q] IN a[q]
    RETURN normalised a
```

For the product of two polynomials, you don't have to use `normalised`, since `plus` always returns a normalised result:

```
HOW TO RETURN a times b:
    PUT {} IN prod
    FOR p IN keys a:
        FOR q IN keys b:
            PUT prod plus {[p+q]: a[p]*b[q]} IN prod
    RETURN prod
```

The *n*-th power of polynomial *a*:

```
HOW TO RETURN a power n:
    CHECK n >= 0 AND n mod 1 = 0 \Positive and integer
    SELECT:
        n = 0: RETURN {[0]: 1}
        n = 1: RETURN a
        n mod 2 = 0:
            PUT a power (n/2) IN b
            RETURN b times b
        ELSE:
            RETURN (a power (n-1)) times a
```

As an example of the use of polynomials, here is the fifth line of Pascal's triangle:

```
>>> WRITE {[1]: 1; [0]: 1} power 4
{[0]: 1; [1]: 4; [2]: 6; [3]: 4; [4]: 1}
```

Here is a simple command to print the result more prettily. Note the method in the for command for traversing the items in reverse order:

```
HOW TO PRINT POLY poly:
   IF #poly = 0: WRITE 0
   FOR i IN {-#poly..-1}:
      PUT -i IN p
      PUT (keys poly) item p IN power
      PUT poly item p IN coef
      IF p <> #poly OR coef < 0:
         WRITE plus.minus[sign coef]
      IF abs coef <> 1 OR power = 0:
         WRITE abs coef<<1
      IF power > 0: WRITE "x"
      IF power > 1: WRITE power<<1
   WRITE /
plus.minus: RETURN {[1]: " + "; [0]: ""; [-1]: " - "}

>>> PRINT POLY {[1]: 1; [0]: 1} power 4
x4 + 4x3 + 6x2 + 4x + 1
```

To simplify typing polynomials in, we can do the following:

```
>>> PUT {[1]: 1} IN x
>>> PUT {[0]: 1} IN one
>>> PRINT POLY (x plus one) power 4
x4 + 4x3 + 6x2 + 4x + 1
```

As another example, we know from school that $(x+1)^2 = x^2+2x+1$ and that $(x+1)(x-1) = x^2-1$:

```
>>> PRINT POLY (x plus one) power 2
x2 + 2x + 1
>>> PRINT POLY (x plus one) times (x minus one)
x2 - 1
```

Now some more operations on polynomials. The derivative:

```
HOW TO RETURN derivative a:
   PUT {} IN result
   FOR p IN keys a:
      IF p <> 0: PUT p*a[p] IN result[p-1]
   RETURN result
```

The integral is similar. Strictly speaking, you also have to give an initial constant, but that can be added in separately.

```
HOW TO RETURN integral a:
   PUT {} IN result
   FOR p IN keys a:
      PUT a[p]/(p+1) IN result[p+1]
   RETURN result
```

It will be useful to be able to convert a number to a constant polynomial:

```
HOW TO RETURN constant c:
   RETURN normalised {[0]: c}
```

Here is a function that evaluates a polynomial when its variable has value x:

```
HOW TO RETURN a at x:
   PUT 0 IN s
   FOR p IN keys a: PUT s+a[p]*x**p IN s
   RETURN s
```

Finally, a function to find a zero of a polynomial, that is a value for its variable such that the value of the polynomial is approximately zero. The parameters u and v are lower and upper limits of where the result must lie; eps gives the accuracy to use: 1e-5 means 5 decimal digits.

```
HOW TO RETURN a zero (u, v, eps):
   \ find a zero of polynomial a, u < zero <= v
   PUT a at u, a at v IN au, av
   CHECK sign au <> sign av \ check zero in the range
   IF au > av: PUT u, v IN v, u
   WHILE abs (u-v) > abs (eps*u):
      PUT ~(u+v)/2 IN mid
      SELECT:
         a at mid < 0: PUT mid IN u
         ELSE: PUT mid IN v
   RETURN v
```

For instance, to find the square root of two using this function, we have to solve $x^2 = 2$, that is $x^2 - 2 = 0$:

```
>>> PUT (x power 2) minus constant 2 IN p
>>> PUT p zero (0, 2, 1e-5) IN r
>>> WRITE r, r**2
1.414215087890625 2.000004314817488
>>> PUT p zero (0, 2, 1e-10) IN r
>>> WRITE r, r**2
1.414213562384248 2.000000000031545
>>> WRITE root 2, (root 2)**2
1.414213562373095 2.000000000000000
```

(What would happen if you tried to find the square root of -1?)

Now for a larger example using these operations. Gravitational acceleration is 9.80665 metres per second squared, downwards:

```
>>> PUT constant -9.80665 IN g
```

If you propel a ball into the air from the ground with an initial vertical velocity of 10 metres per second, then the velocity at any time is expressed by

```
>>> PUT (integral g) plus constant 10 IN velocity
```

so the velocity in metres per second after 1 second is

```
>>> WRITE velocity at 1
0.19335
```

The height of the ball above the ground at any time, in metres, is given by

```
>>> PUT integral velocity IN height
>>> PRINT POLY height
- 4.903325x2 + 10x
```

so the height after 1 second is

```
>>> WRITE height at 1
5.096675
```

How high does the ball go? Well, that is its height when its velocity is zero:

```
>>> PUT velocity zero(0, 100, 1e-5) IN zero.v.time
>>> WRITE zero.v.time
1.0197103023529
>>> WRITE height at zero.v.time
5.09858106471834
```

When does it hit the ground again? When the height is zero:

```
>>> WRITE height zero(1, 100, 1e-5)
2.03942465782165
```

which is what you would expect, namely that it takes twice as long to reach the ground as it does to reach its highest point.

What is its velocity when its height is 3 metres? The time it is at 3 metres is when `height = 3`, or in other words, when `height - 3 = 0`:

```
>>> PUT height minus constant 3 IN h3
>>> PUT h3 zero (0, 1, 1e-5) IN t3
>>> WRITE t3
0.365507125854492
```

and so its velocity at this time is:

```
>>> WRITE velocity at t3
6.41559954423904
```

46   *Examples of ABC*

2.5 SENSE AND SENTENCE

Here are some examples of the use of texts in ABC.

2.5.1 An oracle

This example appears to answer questions with 'yes' or 'no' with some consistency. In fact all it does is output 'yes' if the number of n's in the question is even, and 'no' otherwise. It uses the dyadic version of the operator #, which returns the number of times the first parameter occurs in the second:

```
HOW TO ORACLE:
    READ qn RAW
    WHILE qn <> "":
        WRITE answer[("n"#qn) mod 2] /
        READ qn RAW
answer: RETURN {[0]: "Yes"; [1]: "No"}

>>> ORACLE
Can I ask you a question?
Yes
Are you happy?
Yes
Are you unhappy?
No
Will it rain tomorrow?
No
So I can expect sun?
Yes
And will it stay fine?
Yes
For the whole week?
Yes
```

2.5.2 Eliza

A well known program in the history of computing is 'Eliza' written originally by Joseph Weizenbaum, but since then much imitated by others. It tries to play the role of a psychotherapist: it asks you a question, you reply, it then makes some comment based on your reply, to which you should make some other reply, and so on. It bases its replies only on the structure of your sentence, or on any keywords it can recognise in the sentence. In other words it makes no attempt to 'understand' the sentence.

   This is a simplified version. It only works with keywords, though it could easily

Sense and Sentence 47

enough be beefed up to start recognising some sentence structures. Here is an example of its output; the input lines are preceded by a '>', the rest, in italics, come from Eliza:

> *Hello, I'm Eliza. Tell me about yourself.*
> *(Type "Bye" to finish)*
> \> I'm featuring you in a book
> *Me?*
> \> Yes, I thought you'd be surprised
> *You seem very sure of yourself*
> \> No, I wasn't sure what you'd say
> *Why not?*
> \> Because I was not sure how you would react
> *Not at all?*
> \> I had some vague idea of course
> *Tell me about your problems*
> \> With thousands of people reading this?
> *What a question!*
> *...*
>
> *Let's change the subject*
> \> What shall we talk about?
> *You don't have to ask that!*
> \> That's true
> *What are your interests?*
> \> I work a lot with computers
> *Oh computers! They're so stupid!*
> \> I was afraid you might say that
> *Tell me about your fears*
> *...*

Though this looks quite reasonable, sometimes it can make a real fool of itself by producing a completely unsuitable answer, or by repeating a question you just answered.

The program works by taking each sentence, converting it to lower-case using the ABC function lower:

> \>>> WRITE lower "The moon in June"
> *the moon in june*

and then splitting it into a sequence of words using the ABC function split:

> \>>> WRITE split lower "The moon in June":
> *{[1]: "the"; [2]: "moon"; [3]: "in"; [4]: "june"}*

It then looks to see if the sentence is one of a small number of simple sentences it knows about (such as 'Yes'), for which it has a number of standard answers ('Can you be a bit more specific?'). This is done with a table whose keys are the simple sentences, and whose items are lists of texts.

48   *Examples of ABC*

If that fails, it looks to see if any of the words in the sentence are 'important' keywords that it can use to get you to further expand on, such as 'love', 'fear' or 'family' ('Tell me about your mother'). This is done with a table of words to lists of texts.

Failing this, it looks to see if your sentence was a question (whether it contains a question mark), and if so gives a canned remark (like 'Why do you ask?').

Then it tries with some less important keywords that it can pick up on (like 'never': 'Never is putting it a bit strong isn't it?').

Finally, being unable to get any hints from the sentence at all, it tries to change the subject, again with a canned 'starter' line (such as 'Tell me about your family').

As you can see, it uses no knowledge about the past conversation, and so quickly gets boring, but it is a fun example. Here is the program:

```
HOW TO TALK WITH ELIZA:
   GREET
   LISTEN
   WHILE lower remark <> "bye":
      WRITE reply remark /
      LISTEN
   WRITE "Thank you for talking to me. Bye." /
GREET:
   WRITE "Hello, I'm Eliza. Tell me about yourself." /
   WRITE "(Type ""Bye"" to finish)" /
LISTEN:
   WRITE "> "
   READ remark RAW
```

The function `reply` returns a reply to a remark. It uses five shared permanent datastructures, which it imports with the SHARE command:

```
HOW TO RETURN reply remark:
   SHARE simple, keywords, answers, lesser, starters
   PUT split lower remark IN sentence
   SELECT:
      sentence in keys simple:
         RETURN choice simple[sentence]
      SOME word IN sentence HAS word in keys keywords:
         RETURN choice keywords[word]
      "?" in remark:
         RETURN choice answers
      SOME word IN sentence HAS word in keys lesser:
         RETURN choice lesser[word]
      ELSE:
         RETURN choice starters
```

You might try programming this in another language, to see how it compares in length.

By the way, notice that `simple` is a table whose keys are tables. When first learning ABC it seems unlikely that such a combination would ever occur, but in fact applications do occur quite naturally.

2.5.3 A simple document formatter

The function `split` makes it very easy to make a simple document formatter. For instance with the HELP command earlier, you could type in your lines of help, and let the system worry about filling lines out as fully as possible. This also makes it easier to change help messages: you don't have to worry about the layout of lines.

The formatter works by buffering words up in an output line. If the next word would make the line too long, the output line is written. Additionally, the output line is written if an input line is empty. This gives a simple paragraph facility.

```
    HOW TO FORMAT doc IN width:
       PUT "" IN output
       FOR line IN doc:
          IF line = "": PARAGRAPH
          FOR word IN split line:
             SELECT:
                output = "": PUT word IN output
                word.fits: PUT output^" "^word IN output
                ELSE:
                   FLUSH FULL LINE
                   PUT word IN output
       FLUSH PART LINE
    word.fits:
       REPORT #output+#word < width:
    PARAGRAPH:
       FLUSH PART LINE
       WRITE /
    FLUSH PART LINE:
       WRITE output /
       PUT "" IN output
    FLUSH FULL LINE:
       WRITE output /
```

Examples of ABC

```
>>> FOR nr IN keys paragraph: WRITE nr, paragraph[nr] /
1 The formatter works
2 by buffering words up in an output line.
3 If the next word would make the line too long,
4 the output line is written.
5 Additionally, the output line is written
6 if an input line is empty.
7
8 This gives a simple paragraph facility.


>>> FORMAT paragraph IN 40
The formatter works by buffering words
up in an output line. If the next word
would make the line too long, the output
line is written. Additionally, the
output line is written if an input line
is empty.

This gives a simple paragraph facility.
```

If a document is always going to be used as a sequence of words, then it is worth storing the document not as lines, but as words. For instance, going back to the help example in section 2.3.2, in the command ADD HELP FOR instead of saying

```
APPEND line TO help[topic]
```

saying

```
APPEND split line TO help[topic]
```

In that way `split` gets used only when the document is created, and not each time the document is used.

FORMAT is another possible contender for being a function instead of a command. The advantage is that you can then store the result in a location for later use, you can enquire how many lines are in the result, and so on. The only major difference is that instead of using WRITE each time we produce a new output line, we save it in the result document:

```
HOW TO RETURN width formatted doc:
   PUT {}, "" IN result, output
   FOR line IN doc:
      IF line = "": PARAGRAPH
      FOR word IN split line:
         SELECT:
            output = "": PUT word IN output
            word.fits: PUT output^" "^word IN output
            ELSE:
               FLUSH FULL LINE
               PUT word IN output
   FLUSH PART LINE
   RETURN result
word.fits:
   REPORT #output+#word < width
PARAGRAPH:
   FLUSH PART LINE
   PUT "" IN result[#result+1]
FLUSH PART LINE:
   PUT output IN result[#result+1]
   PUT "" IN output
FLUSH FULL LINE:
   PUT output IN result[#result+1]

>>> DISPLAY 50 formatted paragraph
```
*The formatter works by buffering words up in an
output line. If the next word would make the line
too long, the output line is written.
Additionally, the output line is written if an
input line is empty.*

This gives a simple paragraph facility.

(DISPLAY is in section 2.3.2.)

Finally, let's consider additionally filling each output line with extra spaces so that each full output line spans the width exactly. We can do that by replacing the PUT in FLUSH FULL LINE by an invocation of the function `filled`:

```
PUT width filled output IN result[#result+1]
```

What `filled` has to do is put extra spaces between some words. The total extra space that has to be created is `width-#line`, and this has to be shared between the words on the line. However, this is seldom a whole number of spaces between each word, so for each gap we have to convert the number of spaces to an integer. If we are distributing the extra spaces from left to right and we use floor to convert to integer, the extra spaces will tend to gather at the right hand end; similarly if we use ceiling they will tend to gather at the left hand end. If we use round on the other hand, they will be distributed fairly evenly over the line.

```
HOW TO RETURN width filled line:
   PUT "" IN out
   PUT width-#line, split line IN space, words
   FOR w IN {1..#words}:
      PUT " "^^fill IN gap
      PUT out^(words item w)^gap IN out
      PUT space-(#gap-1) IN space
   RETURN out
fill:
   IF w = #words: RETURN 0 \last word of the line
   RETURN 1+round(space/(#words-w))

>>> DISPLAY 40 formatted paragraph
The formatter  works by  buffering words
up in an output line. If the  next word
would make the line too long, the output
line  is  written.  Additionally,  the
output line is written if an  input line
is empty.

This gives a simple paragraph facility.
```

2.5.4 A cross-referencer

This example takes a document represented as a sequence of lines, and returns a cross-reference index of the document: for each word in the document, the list of lines that the word appears on. It splits each line into words, and then stores the line number in a table under each word:

```
HOW TO RETURN index document:
   PUT {} IN index
   FOR line.number IN keys document:
      TREAT LINE
   RETURN index
TREAT LINE:
   FOR word IN split document[line.number]:
      SAVE line.number IN index AT word
```

(The definition of SAVE is in section 2.2.1.) To output the index, you can use the following; it uses listed from section 2.3.2:

```
HOW TO OUTPUT index:
    FOR word IN keys index:
        WRITE word<<10, listed index[word] /
```

Here it is in use:

```
>>> FOR k IN keys poem:
        WRITE k, poem[k] /
1 I've never seen a purple cow
2 I hope I never see one
3 but I can tell you anyhow
4 I'd rather see than be one

>>> OUTPUT index poem
I          2, 2, 3
I'd        4
I've       1
a          1
anyhow     3
be         4
but        3
can        3
cow        1
hope       2
never      1, 2
one        2, 4
purple     1
rather     4
see        2, 4
seen       1
tell       3
than       4
you        3
```

If the document is stored as words rather than lines, it looks like this:

```
HOW TO RETURN index doc:
    PUT {} IN index
    FOR number IN keys doc:
        FOR word IN doc[number]:
            SAVE number IN index AT word
    RETURN index
```

The surprising thing is, this function is exactly the same (apart from the names used) as the function `inverse` in the telephone list example in section 2.2.1. Why? Well think of an entry in the document as a telephone number (the line number) and a list of people who use that number (the list of words on that line). What we want to produce from a cross-reference is the inverse: for each name (word) the list of telephone numbers for that person (the list of line numbers that word appears on).

You'll notice that the list of words in the index begins with the words starting with a capital letter. This is because the capital letters come before the lower-case letters in the character set. The way to produce the list so that the case of letters does not affect the sorting order, is to store the lower-case version of the word along with the word itself, and alter OUTPUT to ignore the extra word:

```
HOW TO RETURN index doc:
    PUT {} IN index
    FOR number IN keys doc:
        FOR word IN split doc[number]:
            SAVE number IN index AT lower word, word
    RETURN index

HOW TO OUTPUT index:
    FOR lword, word IN keys index:
        WRITE word<<10, listed index[lword, word]/
```

```
>>> OUTPUT index poem
a          1
anyhow     3
be         4
but        3
can        3
cow        1
hope       2
I          2, 2, 3
I'd        4
I've       1
never      1, 2
one        2, 4
purple     1
rather     4
see        2, 4
seen       1
tell       3
than       4
you        3
```

The index of this book was produced using a similar ABC program.

2.5.5 Imitation

This program takes a document in any language and analyses it by recording all pairs of letters, or triplets, or quadruplets etc., depending on a parameter, that occur in the text. It then produces a randomly generated new text based on the old one by only using those tuples recorded. The nice thing is that the new text bears some resemblance to the old one, while being complete nonsense.

To do this, it uses a table to store for each group of $n-1$ characters those characters that can follow the group. So for instance, in the phrase '*taking three as the subject to reason about*', using groups of two letters, the group "re" can be followed by "a" and "e" (from 'three' and 'reason'), so in this case followers["re"] will be {"a"; "e"}. Similarly, followers[" t"] would be {"a"; "h"; "h"; "o"}.

```
HOW TO IMITATE document USING n TUPLES:
    GENERATE IMITATION FROM n analysed document

HOW TO RETURN n analysed document:
    PUT " "^^(n-1), {} IN group, followers
    FOR line IN document: ANALYSE LINE
    RETURN followers
ANALYSE LINE: \ Treating end of line as a space
    FOR character IN line^" ":
        SAVE character IN followers AT group
        UPDATE group WITH character

HOW TO UPDATE group WITH character:
    PUT (group^character)@2 IN group
```

A new text is generated from this table by choosing a random start with choice and choosing a random follower for that group. This follower character is written, and the new group is constructed from the old group and the new character:

```
HOW TO GENERATE IMITATION FROM followers:
    PUT choice keys followers IN group
    WHILE group IN keys followers:
        GENERATE ONE CHARACTER
    WRITE /
GENERATE ONE CHARACTER:
    PUT choice followers[group] IN character
    WRITE character
    UPDATE group WITH character
```

Here are some examples of its output with $n = 1, 2, 3, 4, 5$, using as document the first paragraph of this section:

56 Examples of ABC

With $n=1$:

   xuwoosr.,eimtotrr t uTxhd eleo dteaeesaebsen aesbetedenst en tt auyarl he-cyeesiedtrtrr nai.rotudto,r taa reigni oniee tugnlaouns odi esgpnt ooeot asp peonii n xa cnihels xtateenle Tteeadn trtltuneohrh dd,h rnsh eounisne

With $n=2$:

   The led oring paketesew ord sinecusirdext thin e bairs, las It rs omed pewhing os or be ran tenets, occ. by ce blys gra a ol olyse. bamer, tuproge thiny ts ones r oleply te adedor le omerorakese t tuce w indonon

With $n=3$:

   The thilets programete none te being inguage old or quadruples old onsed occur that the ne, old nice the recor the onses recordin pairs, old onew to this a theneram text bears, whin thending onew text.

With $n=4$:

   The nice thing one, while being those text in thing all pairs of lets, or quadruplets, or quadruplets etc., depending is the tuples it based one by on analyses it based one, while by only using on a rand analyses resemblanguage analyses recorded.

With $n=5$:

   The new text in any language and analyses it by recording is that the old one by only using all pairs of letters, or quadruples recording those tuples recording on a parameter, that the old on a parameter, that then produces a text bears some resemblance thing on then program takes a randomly generated new text in any language and analyses it by only using all pairs of letters, or triplete nonsense.

You can also generate sentences using groups of words rather than characters. Most of the program is the same, the main difference is appending words to the group. A group is most easily held as a sequence of words. Appending a word then looks like this:

```
HOW TO APPEND WORD w TO group:
    FOR k IN keys group:
        PUT group[k] IN group[k-1]
    PUT w IN group[max keys group]
    DELETE group[min keys group]
```

The words are moved up so that groups containing the same words have the same keys and so are identical.

Here is a small sample of output using $n=3$, on a draft of this chapter as input:

   To add a node to the end of the number of dots, and then splitting it into words using the same item (which makes them what are called bags or multisets). Using lists to represent them. The following functions return the union, intersection and difference of two letters, the group "re" can be represented as a sequence of numbers. These numbers are the keys of the words in the sequence is either defined in another entry in the sentence is one of a sequence only works with keywords, though it could easily enough be beefed up to start recognising some sentence structures.

2.5.6 Generating sentences

Here is a simple program that generates random sentences from a template, a grammar. The grammar consists of a table, mapping words to lists of sequences of words. Each of these sequences is an alternative definition for the word being defined. Each word in the sequence is either defined in another entry in the table, or otherwise is to be treated literally.

For instance, suppose a sentence was defined as 'I love GIRL', and GIRL was defined as 'Mary' or 'Anne', and none of the other words was defined. Then we would have the following table:

```
{["Sentence"]: {{[1]: "I"; [2]: "love"; [3]: "GIRL"}};
 ["GIRL"]: {{[1]: "Mary"}; {[1]: "Anne"}}
}
```

This is difficult to read, so here's a command to display it more readably:

```
HOW TO DISPLAY GRAMMAR g:
   FOR defined.word IN keys g:
      WRITE defined.word, ":" /
      FOR alternative IN g[defined.word]
         WRITE "   ", " " listed alternative /

>>> DISPLAY GRAMMAR loves
GIRL:
    Mary
    Anne
Sentence:
    I love GIRL
```

A slightly more involved grammar is:

```
>>> DISPLAY GRAMMAR a.loves.b
BOY:
    Mark
    David
GIRL:
    Hannah
    Anne
Sentence:
    BOY loves GIRL
    GIRL loves BOY
```

58 *Examples of ABC*

To input a grammar, you could use the following command:

```
HOW TO INPUT grammar:
   PROMPT "Define: " FOR term
   WHILE term <> "":
      DEFINITION
      PROMPT "Define: " FOR term
DEFINITION:
   PROMPT "Alternative: " FOR alt
   WHILE alt <> "":
      SAVE split alt IN grammar AT term
      PROMPT "Alternative: " FOR alt
```

which uses the following:

```
HOW TO PROMPT p FOR t:
   WRITE p
   READ t RAW
```

Now given a grammar, here is the command to generate a random sentence from it:

```
HOW TO GENERATE thing FROM sentences:
   SELECT:
      thing in keys sentences:
         FOR word IN choice sentences[thing]:
            GENERATE word FROM sentences
      ELSE:
         WRITE thing, " "


>>> FOR i IN {1..4}:
       GENERATE "Sentence" FROM a.loves.b
       WRITE /
Hannah loves David
Anne loves Mark
Hannah loves David
David loves Anne
```

The quality of the generated sentences depends entirely on the grammar. For instance, here is the basis of a grammar to produce paranoid ramblings:

```
>>> DISPLAY GRAMMAR paranoid
<Sentence>:
    <person> <opines> <something>
    <person> thinks that I am <property>
    I <opine> <something>
    you think that I am <property>
<activity>:
    dancing
    eating
    ...

<object>:
    <person>
    life
    my friends
    ...

<opine>:
    despise
    hate
    ...

<opines>:
    despises
    hates
    ...

<person>:
    my sister
    the man next door
    ...

<property>:
    stupid
    ugly
    ...

<something>:
    <activity>
    <activity> with <person>
    <object>
```

and so on. Here is some output using this grammar:

```
>>> FOR i IN {1..10}:
        GENERATE "<Sentence>" FROM paranoid
        WRITE /
the man next door hates me
my girlfriend hates computers
you think that I am stupid
I despise eating
I am jealous of other people
you think that I am boring
everybody hates walking with my girlfriend
my father thinks that I am ugly
my sister likes computers
I despise my opinions
```

Since earlier we produced a program that imitated a psychotherapist, we can combine the two: first we need to change GENERATE to a function that returns the generated sentence:

```
HOW TO RETURN sentences generated thing:
    SELECT:
        thing in keys sentences:
            PUT "" IN words
            FOR word IN choice sentences[thing]:
                ADD PHRASE
            RETURN stripped words
        ELSE:
            RETURN thing
ADD PHRASE:
    PUT words^" "^(sentences generated word) IN words
```

Now we can write a how-to that lets Eliza and our paranoid talk together to their hearts' content:

```
HOW TO SESSION patient:
    WHILE 1=1:
        PUT patient generated "<Sentence>" IN r
        WRITE "> ", r/
        WRITE reply r/

>>> SESSION paranoid
> you think that I am stupid
Do you think stupidity is a good trait, or a bad one?
> my mother hates jogging
And your father?
> you think that I am ugly
Me?
> my girlfriend thinks that I am stupid
```

How do you get on together?
> my father loves kissing with my girlfriend
Tell me more about your family
> I like relationships
What are your interests?
> you think that I am boring
Boredom is only in the mind
...

CHAPTER 3

Using ABC

3.1 INTRODUCTION

This chapter is an introduction to using the ABC system: how to type in ABC programs, change them, and run them.

Throughout the chapter, the notation [accept] is used to represent the operation *accept*. This isn't an actual key on the keyboard, but represents whatever key is used for the accept operation, since different computers have different keyboards, and since anyway you can decide for yourself which key is used for which operation. Pressing [help] gives you a quick summary of all operations and the keys you use for them. Typing '?' will always give you this summary as well, except if you are typing where a question mark is allowed (in a text or comment).

How you can change which key means what is described in the appendix on the implementations.

3.2 TYPING TO ABC

The first response you get from the ABC system when you start it up is a prompt that looks like this:

>>> ?

The underlined question mark is the indication from the ABC system that it is expecting input from you. (In fact, it depends on the sort of screen you have whether it is underlined, displayed in reverse video, or what. In any case it is displayed in some special way, and we shall use underlining here.) When it follows the three arrows >>>, called the *command prompt*, it is expecting you to type in a command. The question mark is called a *hole* and indicates that something should be filled in; the underline is called the *focus* and shows where you are currently working.

3.2.1 Suggestions

You can fill this hole by typing in a WRITE command for instance: you type a W (which you don't have to type in upper-case: the system knows that it may only be upper-case here), and you immediately see:

>>> W?RITE ?

This extra stuff to the right of the focus is a *suggestion*. Most times that you type a W as the first letter of a command, it is because you want a WRITE. Therefore the system suggests this, with an additional hole for the expression that you want to write. If you do want a WRITE (as in this case) you may press (accept) to accept the suggestion — the focus then moves to the first unfilled hole in the command, which in this case is the only one, and you get:

>>> WRITE ?

You can now type an expression and press (newline). The system evaluates the expression, displays the result, and then gives you a new command prompt. Here are a few examples of WRITE commands and their output:

```
>>> WRITE 2+2
4
>>> WRITE root 2
1.414213562373095
>>> WRITE pi
3.141592653589793
>>> WRITE 2**100-1
1267650600228229401496703205375
>>> ?
```

3.2.2 Undoing mistakes

If you make a mistake while typing and spot it before you type (newline), an easy way to correct it is to use (undo). Pressing (undo) takes you back to the situation before you typed the last key (*exactly* that situation, as you will see clearly after a little use). If you type (undo) twice, you will be taken back to the situation as it was two keys ago, and so forth. Think of (undo) as a way of travelling back in time.

So if you meant to type WRITE pi but instead typed WRITE po, you get:

>>> WRITE po?

Now pressing (undo) will give you

>>> WRITE p?

Now you can type the i and the (newline). Repeatedly using (undo) instead will give you the following sequence:

```
>>> WRITE p?
>>> WRITE ?
>>> W?RITE
>>> ?
```

Because of memory constraints, you can only go back a limited number of keystrokes, and in any case only as far as the command prompt (and thus not back to previous commands). You will see other ways to correct mistakes shortly.

If you should use (undo) once (or more times) too often, you can use (redo) to undo the effects of (undo). Almost any operation can be undone with (undo) (exceptions are (exit), (interrupt), and (newline) when it results in an exit), so don't be afraid to experiment — if something goes wrong you can always undo it.

3.2.3 Typing brackets and quotes

If you make a mistake so that the result is illegal ABC, but don't notice before you press (newline) you will get an error message:

```
>>> WRITE root 9+16
*** There's something I don't understand
    WRITE root 9+16
                ^
*** The problem is: ambiguous; use ( and ) to resolve
>>> ?
```

The problem here is that the system doesn't know if you want to apply `root` to 9 or 9+16 and you should use parentheses to show which.

When you type an open bracket, the system automatically supplies the matching closing bracket for you:

```
>>> WRITE root(?)
```

You now type in the expression

```
>>> WRITE root(9+16?)
```

You may now type (newline) ((accept) will take you over the closing bracket, but it is not necessary to do this):

```
>>> WRITE root(9+16)
5
>>> ?
```

You can write any legal ABC value:

66 *Using ABC*

```
>>> WRITE {1..10}
{1; 2; 3; 4; 5; 6; 7; 8; 9; 10}
>>> WRITE "Hello! "^^3
Hello! Hello! Hello!
>>> ?
```

Just as with parentheses, the system automatically supplies the closing brace }, and the closing quote ". In the latter case, where you want to type something after the closing quote you may either use [accept] or type the quote itself, in order to position after it.

3.3 IMMEDIATE COMMANDS

Commands typed as a response to the command prompt (like all those seen up to now) are called 'immediate' commands, since they are executed immediately. Another example is the PUT command. Just as with WRITE, when you type the first letter of the command, the system provides a suggestion:

```
>>> P?UT ? IN ?
```

Again, you use [accept] to go to the first hole:

```
>>> PUT ? IN ?
```

Here you type an expression,

```
>>> PUT root 2? IN ?
```

followed by another [accept] to take you to the second hole:

```
>>> PUT root 2 IN ?
```

where you can type a name, followed by [newline]:

```
>>> PUT root 2 IN a
>>> PUT root 3 IN b
>>> WRITE a
1.414213562373095
>>> WRITE b
1.732050807568877
>>> WRITE a, b
1.414213562373095 1.732050807568877
>>> WRITE a*a, b*b
2.000000000000000 3.000000000000000
>>> ?
```

3.3.1 Permanent locations

The locations that you create in this way, through immediate commands, are called *permanent locations* because if you stop using the system and come back later and start using the system again you will find that they are still there, with the same values as before.

You can find out which permanent locations exist by typing two equals signs after the prompt:

```
>>> ==
a b
>>> PUT "hello", {1..10} IN message, list
>>> ==
a b list message
>>> WRITE list
{1; 2; 3; 4; 5; 6; 7; 8; 9; 10}
>>> WRITE message
hello
>>> ?
```

3.3.2 Deleting locations

To get rid of locations you no longer want, use the DELETE command:

```
>>> DELETE a, b
>>> ==
list message
>>> WRITE a
*** Can't cope with problem in your command
    WRITE a
*** The problem is: a has not yet received a value
>>> ?
```

As you can see, after the DELETE command both a and b have ceased to exist.

3.3.3 Finishing an ABC session

The one command that has a different meaning when you use it as an immediate command is QUIT, which just terminates the ABC session. When you type the Q you will get a suggestion as usual.

```
>>> Q?UIT
```

Here there are no holes, but you must still accept the suggestion, before pressing (newline).

3.3.4 Other immediate commands

In fact, almost any ABC command can be used as an immediate command; the exceptions are the commands that are only used in how-to's: SHARE, RETURN, REPORT, SUCCEED and FAIL.

```
>>> WRITE list
{1; 2; 3; 4; 5; 6; 7; 8; 9; 10}
>>> INSERT 5 IN list
>>> REMOVE 6 FROM list
>>> WRITE list
{1; 2; 3; 4; 5; 5; 7; 8; 9; 10}
>>> PUT choice list IN number
>>> WRITE number
9
>>> CHECK 9 in list
>>> CHECK 6 in list
*** Your check failed in your command
    CHECK 6 in list
>>> FOR i IN list: WRITE 10*i
10 20 30 40 50 50 70 80 90 100
>>> ==
list message number
>>> ?
```

Note that a CHECK command that succeeds doesn't display any message, and that the location i used in the FOR command doesn't exist afterwards.

3.3.5 Interrupting a running command

If a command is executing, and you want to stop it, pressing [interrupt] aborts the command, giving the message

```
*** interrupted
```

followed by the command prompt. Don't worry if you don't get the prompt immediately; especially with some very long calculations, the system has to clean up some intermediate values before it is ready to accept new input.

3.4 MORE ON TYPING

When you want to type a WHILE command, and you type the initial W, the suggestion you get is of course

>>> W?RITE ?

The system always matches the suggestion to what you have typed, so if you type an H here the system then suggests

>>> WH?ILE ?:

Now you can press (accept) to go to the hole, type the test, and press (newline):

>>> WHILE list <> {}:
           ?

Similarly, to type a READ RAW command, after typing an R, you get

>>> R?ETURN ?

You then type an E and get

>>> RE?AD ? EG ?

You can now accept this suggestion, and type the address:

>>> READ line? EG ?

Now type a (capital) R, and the line becomes:

>>> READ line R?AW

(typing a space followed by a lower-case r has the same effect). Now you can type an (accept) or (newline).

Because ABC matches its suggestions to what you have typed, you can always type the whole command out, letter for letter. Typing WRITE (space) will give you the same result as typing W (accept).

3.4.1 Indentation

Because the ABC system knows that the commands of a WHILE must be indented, it indents for you automatically. So, having typed the first line of a WHILE

>>> WHILE list <> {}:
           ?

you may type in the commands that you want to be part of the WHILE, and each time the system indents you to the right place:

```
    >>> WHILE list <> {}:
            PUT choice list IN number
            REMOVE number FROM list
            WRITE number
            ?
```

After the last command you just need to type an extra (newline), and the system undoes the indentation one level, and executes the WHILE:

```
    >>> WHILE list <> {}:
            PUT choice list IN number
            REMOVE number FROM list
            WRITE number
    2 8 4 7 9 5 3 1 5 10
    >>> WRITE list
    {}
    >>> ?
```

If there is only one simple command to be repeated, it may be on the same line as the WHILE, but doesn't have to be:

```
    >>> WHILE number in list: REMOVE number FROM list
```

3.4.2 Capital letters

As you will have remarked, you hardly ever have to type a capital letter: the ABC system usually knows where a letter must be a capital, and so supplies it for you, even if you don't use the shift key.

However, there are a small number of places where both lower- and upper-case letters are allowed and where you do therefore have to use the shift key, for instance in tests for SOME, EACH, NO, NOT, AND, and OR, and for ELSE. But in any case, you only have to use the shift key for the *first* letter: ABC then knows that the rest of the word must be in upper case.

If you type a command out full, not using (accept), you also have to use the shift key sometimes. For instance, to type PUT a IN b letter for letter, you have to type the I as a capital, since a lower-case i is also allowable after the a.

3.4.3 Redisplaying the screen

Sometimes the screen can get messed up (for instance, if it gets accidentally unplugged). If this happens, or you don't believe what you see on the screen, you can always get confirmation by pressing (look). This causes the screen to be redisplayed.

3.5 THE FOCUS

Apart from (undo), another way of correcting errors is to correct a whole line. Here you use the ability to move the focus about. Up to now, the focus has been a single character, just the hole. However, the focus may be more than one character: it may be several characters, a whole command, or even several commands.

3.5.1 Moving the focus up and down lines

One way of moving the focus is using (upline) and (downline). The operation (upline) moves the focus up to the previous line so that it includes the whole line. Similarly, (downline) moves to the next line. So if you have the following situation:

```
>>> WHILE list <> {}:
        PUT choice list IN number
        REMOVE number FROM list
        WRITE number?
```

then typing (upline) gives you

```
>>> WHILE list <> {}:
        PUT choice list IN number
        REMOVE number FROM list
        WRITE number
```

Here the hole in the last line has disappeared (because the line is legal ABC) and the focus has moved up to the whole of the preceding line. You may press (upline) several times to go up several lines. So, pressing (upline) again gives:

```
>>> WHILE list <> {}:
        PUT choice list IN number
        REMOVE number FROM list
        WRITE number
```

3.5.2 Correcting whole lines

If you have a line that you want to change, you can move the focus to it and press (delete) to get rid of it. This leaves a hole in its place so that you can type a replacement line:

```
>>> WHILE list <> {}:
        ?
        REMOVE number FROM list
        WRITE number
```

If you don't want to replace the line, but completely delete it, then pressing (delete) again deletes the hole too:

72   *Using ABC*

```
>>> WHILE list <> {}:
        REMOVE number FROM list
        WRITE number
```

Remember that [undo] works with *any* operation, so if you accidentally delete the wrong piece of text, [undo] will bring it back again.

3.6 MAKING YOUR OWN COMMANDS

You can create your own commands by typing in a how-to that defines what you want your command to do. In response to the ABC prompt, type an h:

```
>>> H?OW TO ?:
```

type [accept]:

```
>>> HOW TO ?:
```

and type GREET followed by [newline]. This creates a new how-to called GREET (if you are using a machine with a slow disk like a floppy you'll notice some disk activity here as the system writes some information to disk), and the line you just typed is redisplayed against the left edge of the screen (this is to give you the longest possible line length). Notice that the system supplies the indentation for you, just as with WHILE:

```
HOW TO GREET:
    ?
```

You can now type commands to define what GREET should do. For instance, type WRITE "Hello" in the normal way, followed by [exit] or by repeatedly typing [newline] until you get the command prompt again. (An exit, by the way, can't be undone.)

```
HOW TO GREET:
    WRITE "Hello"
>>> ?
```

You give your own commands just as with built-in commands by typing its name after the prompt. You will notice that after typing the G you will get a suggestion for it:

```
>>> G?REET
```

Just as with QUIT, there are no holes, but you must [accept] the suggestion.

```
>>> GREET?
```

Now press [newline] and your command gets executed, and you get the prompt again:

Making your own Commands 73

```
>>> GREET
Hello
>>> ?
```

You may use your own commands just like any built-in command:

```
>>> FOR i IN {1..10}: GREET
HelloHelloHelloHelloHelloHelloHelloHelloHelloHello
>>> ?
```

If the command you define has parameters, you get holes in the suggestion, just as with normal commands. For instance, suppose you prefer LET a BE 10 to ABC's PUT 10 IN a. Well, then you can define the following how-to:

```
HOW TO LET a BE b:
    PUT b IN a
```

Now typing an L, you get the following:

```
>>> L?ET ? BE ?
```

You can then use (accept) in the usual way.

3.6.1 Functions

You make a function in the same way. You type h:

```
>>> H?OW TO ?:
```

and (accept):

```
>>> HOW TO ?:
```

then r:

```
>>> HOW TO R?ETURN ?:
```

and (accept) again:

```
>>> HOW TO RETURN ?:
```

and then, for instance, reversed t, followed by (newline):

```
HOW TO RETURN reversed t:
    ?
```

Now type the following commands, followed by (exit):

```
HOW TO RETURN reversed t:
   IF t = "": RETURN ""
   RETURN (reversed(t@2)) ^ t|1
>>> ?
```

74 *Using ABC*

Now you can use this function like the built-in functions of ABC:

```
>>> WRITE reversed "deliver"
reviled
>>> WRITE reversed "emit"
time
>>> WRITE reversed reversed "emit"
emit
>>> ?
```

3.6.2 Predicates

Predicates (how-to's that test a condition) are created in just the same way. Type h:

```
>>> H?OW TO ?:
```

[accept]:

```
>>> HOW TO ?:
```

r:

```
>>> HOW TO R?ETURN ?:
```

e:

```
>>> HOW TO RE?PORT ?:
```

and [accept]:

```
>>> HOW TO REPORT ?:
```

Now you can type, for instance, palindromic t and [newline]:

```
HOW TO REPORT palindromic t:
   ?
```

and then the body of the how-to:

```
HOW TO REPORT palindromic t:
   REPORT t = reversed t

>>> CHECK palindromic "madam"
>>> CHECK palindromic "rats live on no evil star"
>>> CHECK palindromic ""
>>> CHECK palindromic "I"
>>> CHECK palindromic "madman"
*** Your check failed in your command
       CHECK palindromic "madman"
```

3.6.3 Refinements

Refinements come after the commands of the body of a how-to. For example, suppose you have typed this:

```
HOW TO ORACLE:
   INPUT
   WHILE more:
      OUTPUT
      INPUT
   ?
```

pressing (newline) reduces the indentation one level:

```
HOW TO ORACLE:
   INPUT
   WHILE more:
      OUTPUT
      INPUT
?
```

and pressing (newline) again gives a suggestion for a refinement:

```
HOW TO ORACLE:
   INPUT
   WHILE more:
      OUTPUT
      INPUT
?: ?
```

Type the name (if it is to be in upper-case, you must type at least the first letter of the name in upper-case), followed by (accept) or (newline):

```
HOW TO ORACLE:
   INPUT
   WHILE more:
      OUTPUT
      INPUT
INPUT: ?
```

You can now type in the command or commands of the refinement. More refinements can follow the first in the same way:

76 *Using ABC*

```
            HOW TO ORACLE:
               INPUT
               WHILE more:
                  OUTPUT
                  INPUT
         INPUT: READ qn RAW
         ?: ?

            HOW TO ORACLE:
               INPUT
               WHILE more:
                  OUTPUT
                  INPUT
         INPUT: READ qn RAW
         more: REPORT qn <> ""
         OUTPUT: WRITE ans[which]
         which: RETURN ("n" # qn) mod 2
         ans: RETURN {[0]: "Yes"; [1]: "No"}
         ?: ?
```

Now you can type (newline) to exit.

```
         >>> ORACLE
         Are you happy?
         Yes
         Are you unhappy?
         No

         >>> ?
```

3.6.4 Making changes

Just as you can type two equals signs to find out what permanent locations you have, you can type two colons to find out what how-to's you have. This gives you a list of the first line of each how-to:

```
         >>> ::
         HOW TO GREET:
         HOW TO LET a BE b:
         HOW TO ORACLE:
         HOW TO RETURN reversed t:
         HOW TO REPORT palindromic t:
         >>> ?
```

If you want to visit one, to change it or just to look at its definition, you can type a colon followed by its name, for instance:

>>> :GREET

(you have to type the first letter in upper-case for command how-to's), or:

>>> :reversed

If the how-to you want to visit is the last one you typed in or changed, or the last how-to that you got an error message about, then you don't even need to type its name: the system remembers its name, so all you need to do is type a single colon. The system also gives you suggestions for the names of command how-to's.

What happens now is that the whole how-to (or as much as will fit on the screen if it is big) is displayed with the focus on the line you were last at. You can now move the focus to the lines you want to change, and change them. When you have finished, you use exit.

If a how-to gets so large that it doesn't all fit on the screen, then the ABC system displays as much of it as possible and displays a bar on the bottom line of the screen to indicate which part of it is visible. For instance, this would show you that you are looking at roughly the middle third of the how-to:

------------############------------

3.6.5 Correcting errors

If you type in or change a how-to and the result has an error in it, you will get an error message from the ABC system. This may happen when you press exit, or when you run the how-to, depending on what sort of error it is. For instance in this function, the operand is x, but n is used instead:

```
>>> HOW TO RETURN square x:
        RETURN n*n

>>> WRITE square 4
*** Can't cope with problem in line 2 of square
        RETURN n*n
*** The problem is: n has not yet received a value
>>> ?
```

When you get such a message, it is very easy to make the necessary correction: since the how-to you want to change is the last one that you got an error message for, you only need to type a colon after the prompt:

```
>>> :
HOW TO RETURN square x:
    RETURN n*n
```

As you see, you are positioned at the line that gave the error message. Now you can either press (delete) and retype the whole line, or move the focus to the part that is in error, and deal only with that. How you do that is described shortly.

When typing in or correcting a command or how-to, if you press (exit) and there are still unfilled holes, the system tells you so, and you must fill or delete them.

3.6.6 Renaming and deleting how-to's

You can change the name of a how-to, and the number of parameters, by changing its heading (for instance by deleting the first line, and retyping it). So, renaming GREET into HELLO, and then giving a : : command would give:

```
>>> ::
HOW TO HELLO:
HOW TO LET a BE b:
HOW TO ORACLE:
HOW TO RETURN reversed t:
HOW TO RETURN square x:
HOW TO REPORT palindromic t:
>>> ?
```

If you delete the *whole* of a how-to (by putting the focus on the last line and repeatedly pressing (delete) to delete each line, or by widening the focus until it is on the whole how-to, and then pressing (delete)) the how-to disappears. (Widening is explained shortly.)

Thus deleting HELLO like this will give you:

```
>>> ::
HOW TO LET a BE b:
HOW TO ORACLE:
HOW TO RETURN reversed t:
HOW TO RETURN square x:
HOW TO REPORT palindromic t:
>>> ?
```

3.7 OTHER FOCUS MOVES

Apart from (upline) and (downline) there are four other groups of focus operations:

(first) and (last) to make the focus smaller,
(widen) and (extend) to enlarge it,
(previous) and (next) to move it sideways, and
(up), (down), (left) and (right) for moving a single hole focus about.

Remember that (undo) works with *any* operation, so if you accidentally use the wrong focus move, (undo) will move it back again.

3.7.1 Making the focus smaller

In the case of the faulty function square above, we want to make the focus smaller by going to the last part of the line.

```
HOW TO RETURN square x:
    RETURN n*n
```

The operation (last) works by narrowing the focus to the last part of what is enclosed. Thus, pressing (last) we see:

```
HOW TO RETURN square x:
    RETURN n*n
```

Pressing (delete) deletes the part in the focus, leaving only a hole:

```
HOW TO RETURN square x:
    RETURN ?
```

Now we can type the correct expression and then press (exit):

```
HOW TO RETURN square x:
    RETURN x*x
>>> ?
```

To give you more of an idea of what (last) does, here is a sequence of them:

```
FOR i IN {1..10}: WRITE i*i
FOR i IN {1..10}: WRITE i*i
FOR i IN {1..10}: WRITE i*i
FOR i IN {1..10}: WRITE i*i
FOR i IN {1..10}: WRITE i*i?
```

The operation (first) narrows the focus to the first enclosed part of the focus. Consider the following function:

```
>>> HOW TO RETURN all.chars:
        WRITE {" ".."~"}
>>> WRITE all.chars
*** There's something I can't resolve in all.chars
        WRITE {" ".."~"}
*** The problem is: function returns no value
>>> ?
```

The problem is WRITE has been used, when it should have been RETURN, since this is a function how-to, and not a command. So, we type a colon after the prompt:

```
>>> :
HOW TO RETURN all.chars:
    WRITE {" ".."~"}
```

Pressing (first) narrows the focus to just the keyword:

```
HOW TO RETURN all.chars:
    WRITE {" ".."~"}
```

Pressing (delete) deletes the focus:

```
HOW TO RETURN all.chars:
    ? {" ".."~"}
```

and now we can type RETURN followed by (exit):

```
HOW TO RETURN all.chars:
    RETURN {" ".."~"}
>>> ?
```

To give you more of an idea what (first) does, here is what happens with a sequence of them:

```
FOR i IN {1..10}: WRITE i*i
FOR i IN {1..10}: WRITE i*i
FOR i IN {1..10}: WRITE i*i
FOR i IN {1..10}: WRITE i*i
?FOR i IN {1..10}: WRITE i*i
```

3.7.2 Making the focus larger

The operation (widen) enlarges the focus to the next larger object. For example, if you have this:

```
>>> PUT {"bread"; "butter"} IN shopping
```

or this:

```
>>> PUT {"bread"; "butter"} IN shopping
```

(widen) gives you

```
>>> PUT {"bread"; "butter"} IN shopping
```

and a (delete) removes both entries:

```
>>> PUT {?} IN shopping
```

Here is a sequence of (widen):

```
FOR i IN {?1..10}: WRITE i*i
FOR i IN {1..10}: WRITE i*i
FOR i IN {1..10}: WRITE i*i
FOR i IN {1..10}: WRITE i*i
FOR i IN {1..10}: WRITE i*i
FOR i IN {1..10}: WRITE i*i
```

The operation (extend) extends the focus to the right if possible, and otherwise to the left. For instance, in the following situation

```
>>> PUT {"bread"; "butter"} IN shopping
```

(extend) gives you

```
>>> PUT {"bread"; "butter"} IN shopping
```

and pressing (delete) deletes the first item:

```
>>> PUT {?"butter"} IN shopping
```

Similarly, if you have this:

```
>>> PUT {"bread"; "butter"} IN shopping
```

(extend) gives you

```
>>> PUT {"bread"; "butter"} IN shopping
```

and (delete) then deletes the second item:

```
>>> PUT {"bread"?} IN shopping
```

Here is a sequence of extends:

```
FOR i IN {?1..10}: WRITE i*i
FOR i IN {1..10}: WRITE i*i
FOR i IN {1..10}: WRITE i*i
FOR i IN {1..10}: WRITE i*i
FOR i IN {1..10}: WRITE i*i
FOR i IN {1..10}: WRITE i*i
FOR i IN {1..10}: WRITE i*i
FOR i IN {1..10}: WRITE i*i
FOR i IN {1..10}: WRITE i*i
FOR i IN {1..10}: WRITE i*i
FOR i IN {1..10}: WRITE i*i
FOR i IN {1..10}: WRITE i*i
```

As you can see, (extend) usually enlarges the focus at a slower rate than (widen).

82   *Using ABC*

3.7.3 Moving the focus sideways

The operation (next) moves the focus to the next object to the right. For instance, to focus on the expression of a PUT command:

```
PUT a*a IN b
```

press (first):

```
PUT a*a IN b
```

and then (next):

```
PUT a*a IN b
```

Here are some examples of (first) and (next) in action:

```
WHILE list <> {}:
    PUT choice list IN number
    WRITE number
    REMOVE number FROM list
```

(first):

```
WHILE list <> {}:
    PUT choice list IN number
    WRITE number
    REMOVE number FROM list
```

(next):

```
WHILE list <> {}:
    PUT choice list IN number
    WRITE number
    REMOVE number FROM list
```

(first):

```
WHILE list <> {}:
    PUT choice list IN number
    WRITE number
    REMOVE number FROM list
```

(next):

```
WHILE list <> {}:
    PUT choice list IN number
    WRITE number
    REMOVE number FROM list
```

[first]:

```
WHILE list <> {}:
   PUT choice list IN number
   WRITE number
   REMOVE number FROM list
```

[next]:

```
WHILE list <> {}:
   PUT choice list IN number
   WRITE number
   REMOVE number FROM list
```

[first]:

```
WHILE list <> {}:
   PUT choice list IN number
   WRITE number
   REMOVE number FROM list
```

[next]:

```
WHILE list <> {}:
   PUT choice list IN number
   WRITE number
   REMOVE number FROM list
```

[first]:

```
WHILE list <> {}:
   PUT choice list IN number
   WRITE n?umber
   REMOVE number FROM list
```

[next]:

```
WHILE list <> {}:
   PUT choice list IN number
   WRITE nu?mber
   REMOVE number FROM list
```

The operations [last] and [previous] work exactly the same as [first] and [next] but in the opposite direction.

3.7.4 Moving a single hole

The operations `up`, `down`, `left` and `right` make a hole before the focus, position on it, and then move it one line up or down, or one character left or right. For example, here is a sequence of `left`:

```
WHILE list <> {}:
WHILE ?list <> {}:
WHILE? list <> {}:
WHIL?E list <> {}:
WHI?LE list <> {}:
WH?ILE list <> {}:
W?HILE list <> {}:
?WHILE list <> {}:
```

Here is a sequence of `down`:

```
WHILE list <> {}:
    PUT choice list IN number
    REMOVE number FROM list
    WRITE number

WHILE list <> {}:
    PUT? choice list IN number
    REMOVE number FROM list
    WRITE number

WHILE list <> {}:
    PUT choice list IN number
    REM?OVE number FROM list
    WRITE number

WHILE list <> {}:
    PUT choice list IN number
    REMOVE number FROM list
    WRI?TE number
```

The operations `right` and `up` work exactly the same, but in the other directions.

3.7.5 Using a mouse

Finally, if your system has a mouse, you can use it to position the focus. Clicking at any position positions the focus on the largest complete thing that begins at that point. So for instance, with

```
WHILE list <> {}:
    PUT choice list IN number
    REMOVE number FROM list
    WRITE number
```

clicking on the W of WHILE will focus on the whole WHILE command; clicking on the l of the first occurrence of list will focus on list <> {}; clicking on the { will focus on {}; clicking on the i of list will focus just on that letter; and so on.

3.8 COPYING AND RECORDING

Quite often you will want to duplicate a piece of program. If the focus is on something other than a hole, (copy) copies whatever is in the focus to what is called the *copy buffer* and lets you know that there is something in the copy buffer by displaying the words [Copy buffer] at the bottom of the screen.

If, however, the focus is on a hole, (copy) copies the contents of the buffer into that hole. The [Copy buffer] message then disappears, though actually the contents of the buffer remain, so you can continue to use it.

Of course, you can only copy something back into a hole where it would fit — for instance, you can't copy a command to where an expression is expected. In that case you would just get a beep.

You can use (copy) for moving things too: focus on what you want, press (copy), press (delete) twice to delete it and the hole that gets left after the first delete, move to where you want, make a hole, and press (copy) again.

For example, suppose you have the following how-to:

```
HOW TO AVERAGE tl:
    PUT 0 IN sum
    FOR x IN tl: PUT sum+x IN sum
    WRITE sum/#tl

>>> AVERAGE {1..3}
2
>>> AVERAGE {1}
1
>>> AVERAGE {}
*** Can't cope with problem in your command AVERAGE
        WRITE sum/#tl
*** The problem is: in i/j, j is zero
>>> ?
```

The WRITE should only be done if tl is not empty, so it must be put in an IF command. So we visit the how-to:

```
>>> :
HOW TO AVERAGE tl:
    PUT 0 IN sum
    FOR x IN tl: PUT sum+x IN sum
    WRITE sum/#tl
```

Press (copy):

```
HOW TO AVERAGE tl:
    PUT 0 IN sum
    FOR x IN tl: PUT sum+x IN sum
    WRITE sum/#tl
[Copy buffer]
```

Press (delete):

```
HOW TO AVERAGE tl:
    PUT 0 IN sum
    FOR x IN tl: PUT sum+x IN sum
    ?
[Copy buffer]
```

Type IF #tl > 0 and (accept):

```
HOW TO AVERAGE tl:
    PUT 0 IN sum
    FOR x IN tl: PUT sum+x IN sum
    IF #tl > 0: ?
[Copy buffer]
```

and then (copy) again:

```
HOW TO AVERAGE tl:
    PUT 0 IN sum
    FOR x IN tl: PUT sum+x IN sum
    IF #tl > 0: WRITE sum/#tl?
```

Making a hole to copy to is straightforward: for instance, a (newline) always makes a hole on a new blank line after the line that the focus was positioned on; (accept) always takes you to the first hole on a line, or if there is no hole on the line, then it makes one at the end of the line; and (left) or (right) makes a hole to the left or right of the first character of the focus.

You can also use (copy) for copying between different how-to's: you visit the one how-to, do the copy, exit, visit the second how-to, and copy the text back.

If the [Copy buffer] message isn't being displayed, that is, if the copy buffer is empty or has at least been copied once, and you (delete) something, whatever you delete is silently put into the copy buffer; similarly if the copy buffer is empty, each immediate command is stored in the copy buffer. Thus if you mis-type an immediate command, you can use (copy) to bring it back, and change it.

You never need to empty the copy buffer. Even if it's got something in it that you don't actually need, another [copy] will always replace it with the new text.

The copy buffer is kept between sessions: if you end the ABC session, and come back later, and start using ABC again, its contents are still there.

Remember that [undo] works with *any* operation, so if you accidentally copy the wrong piece of text, [undo] will uncopy it.

3.8.1 Dealing with brackets and quotes

The ABC system always ensures that you have matching brackets and quotes. This means that you can never insert or delete just one of a pair, but must handle both at once. Inserting is easy: you just focus on what you want to have in brackets:

    PUT root x + 1 IN a

and type an open bracket:

    PUT (?root x)+ 1 IN a

Deleting, you have to copy the contents, delete the whole, and copy the contents back:

    PUT 1+(root x) IN a

[copy] and [widen]

    PUT 1+(root x) IN a

[delete]

    PUT 1+? IN a

[copy]

    PUT 1+root x? IN a

3.8.2 Recording

Sometimes you need to repeat a sequence of keystrokes several times. For instance, if you want to rename a location in a how-to, you have to do it once for each occurrence of the name. An easy way to do this is to *record* a sequence of keystrokes. If you press [record], the message [Recording] appears at the bottom of the screen, and any keys that you type thereafter are processed normally and recorded at the same time, until you press [record] again. Then pressing [play] plays those recorded keystrokes back.

So, for instance, focus on the name you want to change, press [record], press [delete], type the new name, and press [record] again. Then focus on the next occurrence of the name, and press [play].

Keystrokes that cause an error during recording are not recorded.

3.9 WORKSPACES

A workspace is a collection of how-to's and permanent locations. You can have several workspaces. When you first use ABC you are in a workspace called 'first'. To visit another workspace, called programs say, you type '>programs' after the prompt:

```
>>> >programs
>>> ?
```

If the workspace doesn't yet exist, the system creates a new empty workspace with that name before visiting it.
To find out which workspaces you have, you type two >'s:

```
>>> >>
first >programs
>>> ?
```

As you can see, the current workspace is marked.
Any how-to's and locations that you create are kept in the workspace where you are working, and these are different than how-to's and locations with the same name in other workspaces:

```
>>> PUT "greetings" IN message
>>> ==
message
>>> ?
```

Typing a single > after the prompt takes you back to the previous workspace you were in (first in this case), and the name of the workspace is displayed as a reminder:

```
>>> >
>first
>>> ==
list message number
>>> WRITE message
hello
>>> ?
```

When you leave a workspace, if it is empty (i.e. it contains no how-to's and locations) it is deleted:

```
>>> >>
>first programs
>>> >programs
>>> ==
message
>>> WRITE message
greetings
>>> DELETE message
>>> ==

>>> >first
>>> >>
>first
>>> ?
```

You can always recreate it of course by visiting it in the normal way:

```
>>> >programs
>>> ==

>>> >>
first >programs
>>> ?
```

The current workspace and the last visited how-to in each workspace are remembered between sessions. When you restart ABC, you are put in the workspace you were last in, and its name is displayed.

3.9.1 Changing the contents of locations

You may also change the contents of permanent locations in the same manner as changing how-to's. Just as you use a single ':' for visiting how-to's, a single '=' followed by the name of a location will display the contents of the location, and let you make changes. In fact, you may replace the contents by any *expression*. When you press (exit), the expression is evaluated, and if all is ok the value is put in the location.

3.9.2 Moving things between workspaces

To move how-to's and values between workspaces, just use (copy): starting in the one workspace, save whatever you want to move in the copy buffer, visit the destination workspace, and copy the buffer back. If you are copying a whole how-to, create and visit a dummy how-to in the destination workspace (for instance HOW TO X:), delete its contents, and then copy the buffer back.

90   *Using ABC*

3.10 SOME COMMON MISTAKES

Most error messages from ABC are self-explanatory. For instance

```
*** Can't cope with problem in your command
    PUT i+1 IN i
*** The problem is: i has not yet received a value
```

However, there are a couple of cases that need a little elaboration.

3.10.1 Uninitialised locations

```
*** There's something I can't resolve in your command
    INSERT 0 IN list
*** The problem is: list hasn't been initialised
```

Just as you can't add 1 to i until i has been given a value, you can't insert an item in a list until that list has got a value. Even if the initial value should be the empty list, you must explicitly start with it:

```
PUT {} IN list
```

Similarly with tables:

```
*** There's something I can't resolve in your command
    PUT 0 IN table[i]
*** The problem is: table hasn't been initialised
```

You can't add an element to a table until that table has been initialised. Again, if you want to start with an empty table, write

```
PUT {} IN table
```

3.10.2 Incompatible types

The message 'Cannot reconcile the types in your how-to' means that you are trying to use a value in an incompatible way. For instance inserting a text in a list of numbers:

```
*** Cannot reconcile the types in your command
    INSERT "John" IN nlist
*** The problem is: I thought nlist was of type EG {0}
```

The type is displayed as an example type, as you might use in a READ EG. So `""` represents a text, 0 represents a number, {0} represents a list of numbers, and so on.

Incompatible types can occur in a number of ways, for instance, if you use INSERT where you meant PUT, or vice-versa, or if you use the wrong type of value as the key to a table.

The ABC system is reasonably clever at deducing type errors; if somewhere in a how-to you have

```
PUT keys t IN list
```

then it deduces that t is some kind of table, so that if later in the same how-to you have

```
WRITE root t
```

it will complain:

```
*** I thought t was of type EG {[?]: ?}
```

in other words, it can see that it was a table, but doesn't know the type of the keys or items. On the other hand, if in the same how-to, you have

```
WRITE 1 + min list
```

then it can deduce that the keys of t must be numbers, and so will say in the error message for root t:

```
*** I thought t was of type EG {[0]: ?}
```

and so on.

In any case, you should look at what types the locations have in the command at fault, and the other uses of the locations in question, and it will usually be clear what the problem is. Note that you can't use one location for values of different types: in this case you should use different locations.

3.10.3 Ambiguous expressions

If you are used to other programming languages, it is initially very easy to forget the outer pair of parentheses in

```
PUT (sin(x+y))**2 IN z
```

If you leave them out, you get this message:

```
*** ambiguous expression; please use ( and ) to resolve
```

Often you can save a pair of parentheses by reversing the operands:

```
WRITE (max keys t)+1
WRITE 1 + max keys t
```

3.11 AN EXAMPLE

Suppose we want to change the AVERAGE command given earlier so that it uses a separate function that returns the sum of the elements of a list or table. So we start off with

```
HOW TO AVERAGE tl:
    PUT 0 IN sum
    FOR x IN tl: PUT sum+x IN sum
    IF #tl>0: WRITE sum/#tl
```

and want to finish with

```
HOW TO AVERAGE tl:
    IF #tl>0: WRITE (sum tl)/#tl

HOW TO RETURN sum tl:
    PUT 0 IN sum
    FOR x IN tl: PUT sum+x IN sum
    RETURN sum
```

First we have to alter AVERAGE so that it uses the new function:

```
>>> :AVERAGE
HOW TO AVERAGE tl:
    PUT 0 IN sum
    FOR x IN tl: PUT sum+x IN sum
    IF #tl>0: WRITE sum/#tl
```

Press (upline) twice:

```
HOW TO AVERAGE tl:
    PUT 0 IN sum
    FOR x IN tl: PUT sum+x IN sum
    IF #tl>0: WRITE sum/#tl
```

press (extend)

```
HOW TO AVERAGE tl:
    PUT 0 IN sum
    FOR x IN tl: PUT sum+x IN sum
    IF #tl>0: WRITE sum/#tl
```

press (copy) (so that we can re-use the two commands for the body of sum) and then (delete):

```
HOW TO AVERAGE tl:
    ?
    IF #tl>0: WRITE sum/#tl
[Copy buffer]
```

Press ⌈delete⌉ again:

```
HOW TO AVERAGE tl:
    IF #tl>0: WRITE sum/#tl
[Copy buffer]
```

Now we have to alter the WRITE to use the new function: press ⌈last⌉

```
HOW TO AVERAGE tl:
    IF #tl>0: WRITE sum/#tl
[Copy buffer]
```

⌈last⌉

```
HOW TO AVERAGE tl:
    IF #tl>0: WRITE sum/#tl
[Copy buffer]
```

⌈first⌉

```
HOW TO AVERAGE tl:
    IF #tl>0: WRITE sum/#tl
[Copy buffer]
```

Type an open bracket:

```
HOW TO AVERAGE tl:
    IF #tl>0: WRITE (?sum)/#tl
[Copy buffer]
```

Type ⌈right⌉ three times (or ⌈accept⌉ and ⌈left⌉):

```
HOW TO AVERAGE tl:
    IF #tl>0: WRITE (sum?)/#tl
[Copy buffer]
```

and type a space and tl:

```
HOW TO AVERAGE tl:
    IF #tl>0: WRITE (sum tl?)/#tl
[Copy buffer]
```

Now ⌈exit⌉. Now we want to use the copied text to make the new function. Type h:

```
>>> H?OW TO ?:
[Copy buffer]
```

⌈accept⌉:

```
>>> HOW TO ?:
[Copy buffer]
```

Type r:

>>> HOW TO R?ETURN ?:
[Copy buffer]

and (accept) again:

>>> HOW TO RETURN ?:
[Copy buffer]

Type sum tl followed by (newline):

HOW TO RETURN sum tl:
   ?
[Copy buffer]

press (copy):

HOW TO RETURN sum tl:
   PUT 0 IN sum
   FOR x IN tl: PUT sum+x IN sum?

and then (newline):

HOW TO RETURN sum tl:
   PUT 0 IN sum
   FOR x IN tl: PUT sum+x IN sum
   ?

Type r:

HOW TO RETURN sum tl:
   PUT 0 IN sum
   FOR x IN tl: PUT sum+x IN sum
   R?ETURN ?

(accept):

HOW TO RETURN sum tl:
   PUT 0 IN sum
   FOR x IN tl: PUT sum+x IN sum
   RETURN ?

Type sum and then (exit).

HOW TO RETURN sum tl:
   PUT 0 IN sum
   FOR x IN tl: PUT sum+x IN sum
   RETURN sum
>>> ?

3.12 SUMMARY OF OPERATIONS

?	display help summary
:name	visit a how-to
:	visit last how-to
::	list how-to's
=name	visit a permanent location
=	visit last permanent location
==	list permanent locations
>name	visit a workspace
>	visit last workspace
>>	list workspaces
QUIT	end session

⎡up⎦ ⎡down⎦ ⎡left⎦ ⎡right⎦: Make the focus a hole, and go one line up or down, or one character left or right.

⎡upline⎦ ⎡downline⎦: Move the focus to the whole line above or below.

⎡previous⎦ ⎡next⎦: Move the focus to the preceding or following object.

⎡widen⎦: Enlarge the focus to the next enclosing object.

⎡extend⎦: Enlarge the focus to the right, or if this is not possible, to the left.

⎡first⎦ ⎡last⎦: Reduce the focus to the first or last enclosed object.

⎡delete⎦: Delete the focus. If the copy buffer is empty, silently save the contents of the focus there.

⎡copy⎦: If the focus is more than a hole, copy its contents to the copy buffer. If the focus is a hole, copy the contents of the copy buffer into the hole.

⎡accept⎦: Move the focus to the first hole on the first line that the focus is in, or to after the first enclosing closing parenthesis, brace or quote, whichever comes first, or otherwise to the end of the line.

⎡newline⎦: Go to a new line, or if on an empty line, decrease the indentation one level, or otherwise do an ⎡exit⎦.

⎡undo⎦: Undo the effect of the last key stroke, whatever it was (except ⎡interrupt⎦ and ⎡exit⎦ or a ⎡newline⎦ that causes a visit or an exit, and ⎡undo⎦ itself).

⎡redo⎦: Undo the effect of the last ⎡undo⎦.

`record`: Start recording all keystrokes typed. If already started, stop recording.

`play`: Play recorded keystrokes back.

`look`: Redisplay screen.

`help`: Display which keys are used for which operation.

`exit`: Exit current how-to, or command (can't be undone).

`interrupt`: Interrupt running command (can't be undone).

3.12.1 Running ABC non-interactively

On some systems, you can also run ABC non-interactively. In this case ABC commands and data are read from the standard input. You may only use normal ABC commands in this case: no focus moves, or changing operations, and no : :, ==, and >> commands.

CHAPTER 4

Description of ABC

4.1 GENERAL ISSUES

This chapter gives a semi-formal definition of ABC. It describes the syntax and semantics of ABC, and lists the predefined commands, functions and predicates.

4.1.1 Values in ABC

ABC has two basic types of values: numbers and texts, and three ways of making new types of values from existing ones: compounds, lists and tables. Texts, lists and tables have in common that they contain an arbitrary length progression of 'items', all of the same type. They are collectively known as *trains*.

All values of a given type have an ordering, which means that all values of the same type can be compared with each other. This ordering is informally specified below; for a precise definition see section 4.6.1, Order tests. Comparison of values of different types is not allowed. All values have a textual representation, and can be written and read.

The built-in functions of ABC for operating on values are described in section 4.4.5, Formulas with predefined functions. Several of these functions are defined for trains in general.

Numbers

Numbers come in two kinds: exact and approximate. Exact numbers are rational numbers. For example, 1.25 = 5/4, and (1/3)*3 = 1. There is no restriction on the size of numerator and denominator. An exact number with a denominator of 1 is referred to as an *integer*.

Approximate numbers are implemented by whatever the hardware or software has to offer for fast but approximate arithmetic (floating point).

The arithmetic operations and many other functions give an exact result when their operands are exact, and an approximate result otherwise, but the function sin, for example, always returns an approximate number.

An exact number can be made approximate with the ~ function (e.g. ~1.25); the functions `exactly, round, floor` and `ceiling` can be used to convert an approximate number to an exact one. Exact and approximate numbers may be mixed in arithmetic, as in 4 * arctan 1, and in comparisons, as in sin x > 0.

Texts

A text (string) is composed of printable ASCII characters, its *items*. Texts are variable length, and are ordered in the usual lexicographic way: "a" < "aa" < "b". There is no separate type 'character': a single character is in fact again a text, of length one.

The printable characters are the 95 characters represented below, where the blank space preceding '!' stands for the (otherwise invisible) space character:

```
 !"#$%&'()*+,-./0123456789:;<=>?
@ABCDEFGHIJKLMNOPQRSTUVWXYZ[\]^_
`abcdefghijklmnopqrstuvwxyz{|}~
```

The ordering on the characters is the ASCII collating order, which is the order in which the characters are displayed above.

Compounds

A compound consists of a sequence of values, its *fields*. For example, the number 3 and the text "xyz" may be combined to give the compound 3, "xyz". Compounds are also ordered lexicographically, For example (3, "xyz") < (3, "yz") < (pi, "aaa").

For this to be meaningful, the compounds that are compared must be of the same type. This means that they have the same number of fields, and that corresponding fields are of the same type.

The only way to obtain the individual fields of a compound is to put it in a multiple-location with the right number of components, as in

    PUT name IN last.name, first.name, middle.name.

Lists

A list is a *sorted* sequence of values, its *items*. All items of a list must be of the same type, and this determines the type of the list. The length of a list may vary without influencing its type. When a new item is inserted in a list (with an INSERT command), it is automatically inserted in the list in the proper position in the sorting order. A list may contain duplicates of the same item. Items may be removed with the REMOVE command. Again, lists themselves are ordered lexicographically.

Tables

A table consists of a (sorted) sequence of *table entries*. Each table entry is a pair of two values: a *key* and an associated value, the corresponding *item*, and the sorting of the entries in the table is on the keys. The ordering of tables is again lexicographic. All keys of a table must be of the same type; similarly, all table items must also be of the same type (but that type may be different from that of the keys). A table may not contain duplicate keys. If `k` is a key of the table `t`, then `t[k]` selects the corresponding item. New entries in a table can be made, or the item of existing entries modified, by putting a new item value in the table after selecting with the key value, as in `PUT a IN t[k]`. Entries can be deleted with the `DELETE` command, as in `DELETE t[k]`. When a table is used as a train, only its items count, and its keys are irrelevant, but the *order* of the items in the train is the same as that of the entries, which are in the order of the sorted keys.

4.1.2 Syntax description method

The syntax of ABC is given in the form of a collection of rules. Each rule is displayed in a box and starts with the name of the thing being defined followed by a colon; following this, one below the other, are one or more alternatives, each clearly marked with a • in front. Each alternative is composed of symbols that stand for themselves, or the names of other rules. These other rules are then defined elsewhere in the grammar, or possibly in the same rule.

Occasionally, a syntax rule is explained in English, rather than formally. Italic font is used for such an explanation.

As an example, here is a simple grammar for a small part of English:

---

sentence:
- declarative
- declarative , connective sentence

---

declarative:
- collective-noun verb collective-noun
- collective-noun do not verb collective-noun

---

collective-noun:
- `cats`
- `dogs`
- `people`
- `the police`

---

verb:
- love
- hate
- eat
- hassle

connective:
- and
- but
- although
- because
- yet

The first rule of this modest grammar states that each sentence is either a declarative, whatever that may be, or a declarative followed by a comma-sign followed by a connective followed by another sentence. What a declarative is, follows from the next rule, and so on, until only symbols remain which need no further explanation. So, one possible sentence can be obtained as follows:

sentence

declarative

collective-noun do not verb collective-noun

dogs do not love the police

Other sentences that can be produced with the grammar are:

```
the police hassle dogs
cats do not hate cats , but cats hate dogs ,
    because dogs hate cats
people eat dogs , yet dogs love people
```

You will notice that the names of rules are in another typeface than words like eat that stand for themselves. In the grammar of ABC that follows, furthermore, rule names are all in lower-case letters, while words that stand for themselves, with one exception, are all in upper-case letters, so they are easily distinguished. The one exception is the letter e in the exponent part of a numeral in section 4.4.1.

It often happens that a part of an alternative is optional. There is a special template rule serving for all these cases:

General Issues 101

> optional-*whatever*:
> • empty
> • *whatever*

> empty:
> •

(Empty produces nothing.)

The 'optional' rule is included to save many rules in the definition, and stands for rules like:

> optional-comment:
> • empty
> • comment$_{1.3}$

If a name is used in a rule whose definition is to be found in another section, then the sub-section number is appended in small print for easy reference, omitting the '4'. For instance the rule above indicates that the rule for comment is to be found in section 4.1.3.

4.1.3 Representations

> new-line:
> • optional-comment new-line-proper
>   indent

ABC program texts consist of indented lines. A new-line-proper marks a transition to a new line. An indent stands for the left margin blank offset. Initially, the left margin has zero width. The indentation is increased by an increase-indentation and decreased again by a decrease-indentation. These always come in pairs and serve for grouping, just as begin-end pairs do in other programming languages. An increase-indentation is always preceded by a line ending with a colon (possibly followed by comment).

> comment:
> • \ optional-comment-body

Comments may be placed at the end of a line or may stand alone on a line where a command may otherwise stand. No comment may precede the first line of a how-to (see section 4.2).

> comment-body:
> - printable-character$_{1.1}$ optional-comment-body

Example comment:

```
\modified 6/4/84 to reject passwords of length < 6
```

Lines are constructed from *signs* organised into *symbols*: keywords, names, numerals, and other symbols.

> keyword:
> - *a sequence of capital letters (A to Z), digits, points (.), and quotes (' and "), beginning with a letter.*

A point in a keyword must not be followed by another point, nor be the last sign of the keyword.

> keyword-suite:
> - keyword optional-keyword-suite

Example keywords: keyword-suites:

    PUSH   PUSH
    CAN'T.DO   CAN'T DO
    UPSIDE   UPSIDE DOWN
    A.3'B"

> name:
> - *the same as* keyword, *except that lower-case letters (*a *to* z*) are used instead of capital letters.*

Example names:

    push
    can't.do
    a.3'b"

Most other symbols consist of single signs, but some are composite: . . , **, */, /*, ^^, <<, ><, >>, <=, <> and >=.

Spaces are freely allowed between symbols, but not within keywords, names, numerals and composite symbols. Sometimes spaces are required to separate keywords and names from following symbols. For example, cos y is not the same as cosy: the latter is taken to be one name.

4.2 HOW-TO'S

How-to's are the building blocks of an ABC 'program'. You can define new commands, functions and predicates by writing a how-to. These how-to's reside in a workspace.

---
how-to:
- command-how-to$_{2.1}$
- function-how-to$_{2.2}$
- predicate-how-to$_{2.3}$

---
how-to-script:
- command-suite$_3$
    optional-refinement-suite$_{2.4}$

A name used as an address of a location (a variable) in a how-to is by default private (local) to that how-to. This means that if the same name is used as an address outside the how-to, it refers to a different location. So the location for a private name is only accessible during the invocation of the how-to. It is therefore a temporary location that ceases to exist at the end of the invocation. If a location should be shared between several how-to's, or should otherwise survive the invocation in which it is created, either it should be passed as a parameter, or the name should be listed in a share-command (section 4.3.1) at the start of the how-to-script, in which case it then stands for a shared (global) name of the workspace. The location of a shared name is created as 'permanent', meaning that it survives, together with its contents, even on logging out. The shared names with the contents of their locations are also called the 'permanent environment'. There is one permanent environment corresponding to each workspace.

The invocation of a function- or predicate-how-to cannot alter the contents of permanent locations or delete them, or create new permanent locations, in any way such that the changes survive after the invocation of the how-to (in other words, such how-to's cannot have 'side-effects'). If such a how-to appears to modify the contents of a shared name, it effectively modifies a private 'scratchpad' *copy*, and the change is invisible after the invocation of the how-to.

4.2.1 Command how-to's

A command-how-to defines the meaning of a new command (see section 4.3.16, User-defined commands, for how to invoke them). Once the command has been defined, it may be used in the same way as the built-in commands of ABC. The execution of the command then invokes the how-to, whose script specifies what actions must be taken for executing the command. Other user-defined commands may be used in the script of a how-to when writing it, even if they have not yet been defined, though they must be defined by the time the how-to is invoked.

command-how-to:
- HOW TO command-template :
    how-to-script$_2$

command-template:
- keyword-suite$_{1,3}$ optional-template-trailer

The first keyword-suite of a command-template must be unique, i.e., different from the first keyword-suites of all predefined and other user-defined commands. So it is impossible to redefine the built-in commands of ABC. Additionally, the very first keyword of the suite may not be CHECK, HOW, IF, REPORT, RETURN or WHILE. Otherwise, it may be chosen freely. There are no restrictions on the second and further keyword-suites.

template-trailer:
- template-parameter
- template-parameter keyword-suite$_{1,3}$ optional-template-trailer

template-parameter:
- naming$_5$

Example command-how-to:

```
HOW TO PUSH value ON stack:
    PUT value IN stack[#stack+1]
```

See also: user-defined-commands (4.3.16).

4.2.2 Function how-to's

A function-how-to defines the meaning of a new function (see section 4.4.5, Formulas with user-defined functions, for how to invoke them).

Functions are used in formulas (4.4.5), which are a special case of expressions. The first line of a how-to defining a new function contains a so-called formula-template, which contains the name of the function being defined. Formulas may be zeroadic (no operands), monadic (one operand following the function name) or dyadic (two operands surrounding the function name). A function-how-to is invoked upon the evaluation of a formula and returns a value, which is supplied with the return-command (section 4.3.12).

function-how-to:
- HOW TO RETURN formula-template :
    how-to-script$_2$

formula-template:
- zeroadic-formula-template
- monadic-formula-template
- dyadic-formula-template

zeroadic-formula-template:
- name$_{1.3}$

monadic-formula-template:
- name$_{1.3}$ template-operand

dyadic-formula-template:
- template-operand name$_{1.3}$ template-operand

Function names must not be 'overloaded' (multiply defined). However, a given name may be used at the same time for a dyadic function and a monadic function.

template-operand:
- single-naming$_5$

Example function-how-to:

```
HOW TO RETURN (a, b) over (c, d):
    PUT c*c+d*d IN rr
    RETURN (a*c+b*d)/rr, (-a*d+b*c)/rr
```

See also: return-commands (4.3.12), formulas with user-defined functions (4.4.5).

4.2.3 Predicate how-to's

A predicate-how-to defines the meaning of a new predicate (see section 4.6.2, Examinations with user-defined predicates, for how to invoke them). Predicates are used in examinations, which are a special case of tests. Like functions, predicates may be zeroadic, monadic or dyadic.
 Tests do not return a value, but succeed or fail via the report, succeed and fail commands.

predicate-how-to:
- HOW TO REPORT examination-template :
    how-to-script$_2$

> examination-template:
> - zeroadic-examination-template
> - monadic-examination-template
> - dyadic-examination-template

> zeroadic-examination-template:
> - $name_{1.3}$

> monadic-examination-template:
> - $name_{1.3}$ $template\text{-}operand_{2.2}$

> dyadic-examination-template:
> - $template\text{-}operand_{2.2}$ $name_{1.3}$ $template\text{-}operand_{2.2}$

Like functions, predicate names must not be 'overloaded', though a given name may be used at the same time for a dyadic predicate and a monadic predicate.

Example predicate-how-to:

```
HOW TO REPORT a subset b:
    REPORT EACH x IN a HAS x in b
```

See also: report-commands (4.3.13), succeed-command (4.3.14), fail-command (4.3.15), examinations with user-defined predicates (4.6.2).

4.2.4 Refinements

Refinements support the method of 'top-down' programming, also known as programming by 'stepwise refinement'. When writing a how-to, the specification of commands, expressions and tests may be deferred by referring them to *refinements* that reflect the appropriate coarse-grained level of the algorithm. These refinements are then specified at the end of the how-to, and may themselves be refined to the necessary detail, possibly in several steps. As with how-to's, there are three kinds of refinements. The differences with how-to's are:

— refinements are private to a how-to and cannot be invoked from other how-to's;
— the private names in the how-to are also known inside its refinements;
— no parameters or operands can be passed to a refinement.

How-to's 107

---

refinement-suite:
- new-line$_{1.3}$
    refinement
    optional-refinement-suite

---

refinement:
- command-refinement
- expression-refinement
- test-refinement

---

command-refinement:
- keyword-suite$_{1.3}$:
    command-suite$_3$

The keyword-suite of a command-refinement must be different from the first keyword-suites of all predefined commands, and of all other command-refinements in the how-to. It may, however, be the same as the first keyword-suite of a user-defined-command. Additionally, the very first keyword of the suite may not be CHECK, HOW, IF, REPORT, RETURN or WHILE.

Example command-refinement:

```
SELECT TASK:
    PUT min tasks IN task
    REMOVE task FROM tasks
```

---

expression-refinement:
- name$_{1.3}$:
    command-suite$_3$

Example expression-refinement:

```
stack.pointer:
    IF stack = {}: RETURN 0
    RETURN max keys stack
```

---

test-refinement:
- name$_{1.3}$:
    command-suite$_3$

Example test-refinement:

```
special.case: REPORT position+d = line.length
```

See also: refined-commands (4.3.17), refined-expressions (4.4.6), refined-tests (4.6.3).

4.3 COMMANDS

Commands may be given as 'immediate commands', interactively from the keyboard, or may be part of a how-to. If commands are given as immediate commands, they are obeyed directly: any names used as addresses in the command are then interpreted as shared names from the permanent environment. Within a how-to, address names are private, unless they have been listed in a share-command (see section 4.3.1).

If the interrupt key is pressed while a command is executing, or a run-time error is reported, execution is aborted, and the user is prompted for another immediate command.

---

command:
- simple-command
- control-command

---

simple-command:
- share-command$_{3.1}$
- check-command$_{3.2}$
- put-command$_{3.3}$
- write-command$_{3.4}$
- read-command$_{3.5}$
- set-random-command$_{3.6}$
- remove-command$_{3.7}$
- insert-command$_{3.8}$
- delete-command$_{3.9}$
- pass-command$_{3.10}$
- terminating-command
- user-defined-command$_{3.16}$
- refined-command$_{3.17}$

---

terminating-command:
- quit-command$_{3.11}$
- return-command$_{3.12}$
- report-command$_{3.13}$
- succeed-command$_{3.14}$
- fail-command$_{3.15}$

---

control-command:
- if-command$_{3.18}$
- select-command$_{3.19}$
- while-command$_{3.20}$
- for-command$_{3.21}$

> command-suite:
> - simple-command
> - increase-indentation
>   command-sequence
>   decrease-indentation

Command-suites are used in the bodies of how-to's, refinements, and control-commands. A command-suite may only follow the preceding colon on the same line if it is a simple-command. Otherwise, it starts on a new line, with all lines of the command-suite indented.

> command-sequence:
> - new-line$_{1,3}$
>   command
>   optional-command-sequence

Example command-suite:

```
IF name in keys abbrev.table:
    PUT abbrev.table[name] IN name
IF name not.in name.list:
    INSERT name IN name.list
```

The commands of a command-suite are executed one by one, until the last one has been executed or until a terminating command (see section 4.3) is executed.

The execution of the command-suite of a function-how-to or expression-refinement must end in a return-command, and return-commands may only occur within such command-suites.

The execution of the command-suite of a predicate-how-to or test-refinement must end in a report-, succeed- or fail-command, and these may only occur within such command-suites.

4.3.1 SHARE

Share-commands are used to import shared names into a how-to.

> share-command:
> - SHARE naming$_5$

A share-command may only occur as the first command of a how-to, or immediately after another share-command.

Example share-command

    SHARE name.list, abbrev.table

The names of the naming are taken as names of non-local permanent locations. Whenever the names are located during the invocation of the how-to, these permanent locations are used instead of temporary locations private to the how-to.

4.3.2 CHECK

Check-commands are used to check that a condition is satisfied. They may be used, for example, to check the requirements of parameters or operands on invoking a how-to. The liberal use of check-commands helps to get programs correct quickly.

---
check-command:
- CHECK test$_6$

Example check-command:

    CHECK i >= 0 AND j >= 0 AND i+j <= n

When a check-command is executed, its test is performed. If the test fails, an error is reported and the currently executing immediate command is aborted. Otherwise, no message is given and execution continues.

4.3.3 PUT

Put-commands are the assignment commands of ABC.

---
put-command:
- PUT expression$_4$ IN address$_5$

Example put-command:

    PUT a+1, ({}, {1..a}) IN a, b

The value of the expression is put in the location of the address, which means that a copy of the value is stored there. If no such location exists already, one is created on the spot. The value will be held in that location until a different value is put in the location, or the location is deleted. It can be inspected again by just naming the right address. The types of the value and the location must agree (though this is currently not always checked).

    If the location is created locally (the name did not occur in an immediate command and was not listed in a share-command), the location will cease to exist when the current how-to is exited. If a location already existed for the name, its old contents are superseded by the new value.

If a value is put in a multiple-location, the value must be a compound with as many fields as there are single-locations in the multiple-location. The successive fields are then put in the successive single-locations. It is an error in such a 'multiple put' if it makes a difference in what order the fields are put in the single-locations (as in PUT 1, 2 IN x, x where the final value of x might be either 1 or 2).

Note that the meaning of PUT a, b IN b, a is well defined (provided that a and b are defined and have values of the same type): first the value of the expression a, b is determined, and then that value is put in b, a. Note also that the meaning of PUT t[i], t[j] IN t[j], t[i] is well defined, even if i and j have the same value. For although in this case a value is put twice in the same location, that value is the same each time, so the order does not matter.

This definition of putting a value in a location is also used by read-commands, for-commands, user-defined-commands, user-defined-functions and -predicates, and quantifications.

See also: delete-commands (4.3.9), addresses (4.5).

4.3.4 WRITE

Write-commands are used to write values on the screen. All values in ABC may be written.

---

write-command:
- WRITE output-format

---

output-format:
- new-liners
- optional-new-liners single-expression-sequence optional-new-liners

---

new-liners:
- / optional-new-liners

---

single-expression-sequence:
- single-expression$_4$
- single-expression$_4$, single-expression-sequence

Example write-commands:

    WRITE //
    WRITE count[k], "times", k /

Each single-expression, if any, is evaluated and converted to a text and written on the screen. Each / causes a transition to a new line on the screen. Note that you write no comma before or after the /'s.

The value of each single expression is converted to a text according to the syntax of single-expression (section 4.4), unless it is a text, when it is converted without surrounding quotes. Adjacent single-expressions are written separated by a space, unless they are texts. Thus,

    WRITE 0, 1, "!", 2, "x", "y", 3, ("x", "y") /

gives

    0 1 ! 2 xy 3 ("x", "y")

and

    WRITE "Yell"
    WRITE "ow!" /

gives

    Yellow!

For formatting purposes, see the operators >>, <<, and >< (section 4.4.5E), the function round (section 4.4.5A), and the conversions in text-displays (section 4.4.4).

4.3.5 READ

Read-commands are used to read input from the user. Values of any type can be read.

---
read-command:
- READ input-format

---
input-format:
- single-address$_5$ EG single-expression$_4$
- single-address$_5$ RAW

Example read-commands:
    READ x EG 0
    READ (n, s) EG (0, "")
    READ message[#message+1] RAW

The execution of a read-command prompts the user to supply one input line.

With an EG format, the input is interpreted as an *expression* of the same type as the example expression following EG. (Usually, the example expression will consist of constants, but other expressions are also allowed.) The input expression is evaluated in the permanent environment (so private names of how-to's cannot be used) and put in the location of the single-address. To input a text-display (literal), text quotes are required.

If a RAW format is specified, the single-address must be a text address. The input line is put in the location of the address literally. No text quotes are needed.

4.3.6 SET RANDOM

Set-random-commands are used to start or re-start the random sequence used for the functions `random` (see 4.4.5A) and `choice` (see 4.4.5D). They can be used, for instance, to make the results from programs using these functions reproducible.

---
set-random-command:
- SET RANDOM expression₄

Example set-random-command:

    SET RANDOM "Monte Carlo", run.nr

The random sequence used for the functions `random` and `choice` is reset to a point depending on the value of the expression (how this is done is not further specified). Each ABC-session starts this sequence at some random point.

4.3.7 REMOVE

Remove-commands are used to remove an item from a list.

---
remove-command:
- REMOVE expression₄ FROM address₅

Example remove-command:

    REMOVE task FROM tasks

The location of the address must hold a list, and the value of the expression must be an item of that list. The item is removed. If it was present more than once, only one instance is removed.

4.3.8 INSERT

Insert-commands are used to insert an item in a list.

---
insert-command:
- INSERT expression₄ IN address₅

Example insert-command:

    INSERT new.task IN tasks

The location of the address must hold a list. The value of the expression is inserted as a list item. If that item was already present, one more instance will be present.

4.3.9 DELETE

Delete-commands are used to delete locations, including those of table entries and other (non-text-selection) addresses such as unwanted shared names and their locations.

> delete-command:
> ● DELETE address$_s$

Example delete-command:

> DELETE t[i], u[i, j]

The location for the address ceases to exist. If a multiple-address is given, all its single-addresses are deleted. If a table-selection-address is given, the table must contain the key that is used as selector. The table entry with that key is then deleted from the table. It is an error to delete a text-selection-address (e.g., t@2).

Note that the meaning of DELETE t[i], t[j] is well defined, even if i and j have the same value.

4.3.10 PASS

A pass-command serves to provide a dummy filling for a command-suite (which may not be empty) in case no action is needed. This is mainly useful in select-commands, but also for the scripts of how-to's still under construction.

> pass-command:
> ● PASS

Example pass-command:

> PASS

The execution of a pass-command entails no action.

Example of the use of a pass-command:

> SELECT:
>   too.small: ENLARGE
>   too.large: REDUCE
>   just.fine: PASS

4.3.11 QUIT

A quit-command is used for terminating the invocation of command-how-to's or command-refinements, or to terminate an ABC session.

> quit-command:
> • QUIT

A quit-command may only occur in the command-suite of a command-how-to or command-refinement, or as an immediate command.

Example quit-command:

> QUIT

The execution of a quit-command causes the termination of the invocation of the command-how-to or command-refinement in whose command-suite it occurs. The execution of the invoking user-defined- or refined-command is thereby terminated and further execution continues as if the invoking command had terminated normally.

Given as an immediate command, QUIT terminates the current session. All how-to's and shared names with their locations in the permanent environment survive and can be used again at the next session.

4.3.12 RETURN

Return-commands are used to terminate the invocation of a function-how-to or expression-refinement, and return a value.

> return-command:
> • RETURN expression_4

Return-commands may only occur within the command-suite of a function-how-to or expression-refinement.

Example return-command:

> RETURN (a*c+b*d)/rr, (-a*d+b*c)/rr

The execution of a return-command causes the termination of the invocation of the function-how-to or expression-refinement in whose command-suite it occurs. The value of the expression is returned as the value of the invoking formula or refined-expression.

4.3.13 REPORT

Report-commands are used to terminate the invocation of a predicate-how-to or test-refinement, reporting success or failure.

> report-command:
> ● REPORT test$_6$

Report-commands may only occur within the command-suite of a predicate-how-to or test-refinement.

Example report-command:

```
REPORT i in keys t
```

The execution of a report-command causes the termination of the invocation of the predicate-how-to or test-refinement in whose command-suite it occurs. The invoking examination or refined-test succeeds/fails if the test of the report-command succeeds/fails. If the invoker is a test-refinement, any bound names set by a for-command (see section 4.3.21) or a quantification (section 4.6.7) will temporarily survive, as described under REFINED-TESTS (section 4.6.3). The command 'REPORT test' is equivalent to

```
SELECT:
    test: SUCCEED
    ELSE: FAIL
```

4.3.14 SUCCEED

A succeed-command is used to terminate the invocation of a predicate-how-to or test-refinement, reporting success.

> succeed-command:
> ● SUCCEED

Succeed-commands may only occur within the command-suite of a predicate-how-to or test-refinement.

Example succeed-command:

```
SUCCEED
```

The execution of a succeed-command causes the termination of the invocation of the predicate-how-to or test-refinement in whose command-suite it occurs. The invoking examination or refined-test succeeds. As with report-commands, bound names temporarily survive.

The command SUCCEED is equivalent to REPORT 1 = 1.

4.3.15 FAIL

A fail-command is used to terminate the invocation of a predicate-how-to or test-refinement, reporting failure.

fail-command:
- FAIL

Fail-commands may only occur within the command-suite of a predicate-how-to or test-refinement.

Example fail-command:

FAIL

The execution of a fail-command causes the termination of the invocation of the predicate-how-to or test-refinement in whose command-suite it occurs. The invoking examination or refined-test fails. As with report-commands, bound names temporarily survive.

The command FAIL is equivalent to REPORT 1 = 0.

4.3.16 User-defined commands

These are commands defined by a how-to.

user-defined-command:
- keyword-suite$_{1.3}$ optional-trailer

trailer:
- actual-parameter
- actual-parameter keyword-suite$_{1.3}$ optional-trailer

actual-parameter:
- address$_5$
- expression$_4$

The keywords and actual-parameters must correspond one to one to the keywords and template-parameters of the command-template of one unique command-how-to in the current workspace.

118   *Description of ABC*

Example user-defined-commands:
```
CLEAN UP
DRINK me
TURN a UPSIDE DOWN
PUSH v ON operand.stack
```

A user-defined-command is executed in the following steps:

1. A modified copy of the command-how-to is made in which any private names in the how-to that might clash with names currently in use are systematically replaced by other names that do not cause conflict.
2. A location is created for each template-parameter of the modified how-to. If, according to the text of the how-to, the execution of its command-suite may cause a value to be put in that location or a component of it, or cause the deletion of it or a component of it, then that parameter is at an 'address position'; otherwise, it is at an 'expression position'.
3. Each actual-parameter is considered. If it is at an address position, it must have the form of an address and it is located. If its location holds a value, the value is put in the location created for the corresponding template-parameter. If the actual-parameter is at an expression position, it is evaluated and its value is put in the location created for the corresponding template-parameter.
4. The command-suite of the modified how-to is executed.
5. Upon the completion of this execution, each template-parameter at an address position is considered. If it has a value, this value is put back in the location of the corresponding actual-parameter. If it has no value, the location of the corresponding actual-parameter is deleted. The same restrictions apply as for 'multiple puts' (see 4.3.3) and for delete-commands (see 4.3.9).
6. It is an error if upon completion of execution, some template-parameter has a multiple-location some but not all of whose components hold a value.

The execution of the user-defined-command is complete when the execution of the command-suite terminates (normally, or because of the execution of a quit-command) and the address positions as described above have been dealt with.

The effect of this parameter passing is as follows: Actual-parameters that are expressions, and expressions contained in an actual-parameter that is an address, are evaluated once, at the entry of the how-to. During the execution of the how-to-script, the template-parameters serve as private names. Only upon completion are values that were put in template-parameters in the course of execution passed back to the actual-parameters. If the execution is aborted by a user-interrupt or because of an error, the actual-parameters will not be affected. Changes to shared names from within the how-to-script, however, take effect immediately.

An example of a call of a how-to that is not allowed due to restriction 6 above is

```
HOW TO FILL HALF OF a, b:
    PUT 0 IN b

PUT {} IN table
FILL HALF OF table[1]
```

Note that in contrast to function- and predicate-how-to's, changes to the template-parameters will be passed back to the actual-parameters of a command, so that they cannot be used as working storage for intermediate calculations.

See also: command-how-to's (4.2.1), quit-command (4.3.11).

4.3.17 Refined commands

These are used to execute commands defined in command-refinements.

---
refined-command:
- keyword-suite$_{1.3}$

The keyword-suite of a refined-command must occur as the keyword-suite of one command-refinement in the how-to in which it occurs. That command-refinement specifies the meaning of the refined-command.

Example refined-command:

```
REMOVE MULTIPLES
```

A refined-command is executed by executing the command-suite of the corresponding command-refinement. The execution of the refined-command is complete when the execution of this command-suite terminates (normally, or because of the execution of a quit-command).

See also: command-refinement (4.2.4), quit-command (4.3.11).

4.3.18 IF

If-commands are used to conditionally execute a command-suite depending on the success of a test. If something should be executed on failure too, or there are more alternatives, a select-command should be used.

---
if-command:
- IF test$_6$:
    command-suite$_3$
---

120 *Description of ABC*

Example if-command:
```
IF i < 0: PUT -i, -j IN i, j
```
The test is performed. If it succeeds, the command-suite is executed; if it fails, the command-suite is not executed.

The command "IF test: command-suite" is equivalent to:
```
SELECT:
    test: command-suite
    ELSE: PASS
```

See also: select-commands (4.3.19).

4.3.19 SELECT

Select-commands are used to conditionally execute one out of a number of command-suites depending on the success of associated tests.

---
select-command:
- SELECT :
    alternative-suite

---
alternative-suite:
- increase-indentation
    alternative-sequence
    decrease-indentation

---
alternative-sequence:
- new-line$_{1.3}$
    single-alternative
    optional-alternative-sequence
- new-line$_{1.3}$
    else-alternative

---
single-alternative:
- test$_6$:
    command-suite$_3$

> else-alternative:
> - ELSE :
>   command-suite$_3$

Example select-commands:

```
SELECT:                      SELECT:
    a < 0: RETURN -a             a < 0: RETURN -a
    a >= 0: RETURN a             ELSE: RETURN a
```

The tests of the alternatives are performed one by one, starting with the first and proceeding downwards, until one is found that succeeds. The corresponding command-suite is then executed. ELSE may be used in the final alternative as a test that always succeeds. If all the tests fail, an error is reported.

4.3.20 WHILE

While-commands are used to execute a command-suite repeatedly, depending on the success of a test.

> while-command:
> - WHILE test$_6$:
>   command-suite$_3$

Example while-command:

```
WHILE x > 1: PUT x/10, c+1 IN x, c
```

If the test succeeds, the command-suite is executed. If the execution of the command-suite terminates normally, the test is performed a second time, and if it succeeds, the command-suite is executed again, and next the test is performed again, and this alternation continues until the test, when performed, fails, or until an escape is forced by a terminating-command. If the test fails the very first time, the command-suite is not executed at all.

4.3.21 FOR

For-commands are used to repeat a command-suite once for each item of a train.

> for-command:
> - FOR ranger :
>   command-suite$_3$

122 *Description of ABC*

> ranger:
> • naming₅ IN expression₄

Example for-commands:

```
FOR i IN {1..10}: WRITE i, i**2 /
FOR k IN keys t: WRITE k, ":", t[k] /
FOR i, j IN keys t: PUT t[i, j] IN t'[j, i]
```

The value of the expression must be a train. One by one, each item of that train is put in the location of the naming, and each time the command-suite is then executed. For example,

```
FOR c IN "ABC": WRITE "letter is ", c /
```

is equivalent to

```
WRITE "letter is ", "A" /
WRITE "letter is ", "B" /
WRITE "letter is ", "C" /
```

If t is a table, then 'FOR a IN t: TREAT a' treats the table items of t in the same way as

```
FOR k IN keys t:
    PUT t[k] IN a
    TREAT a
```

Note that the expression of a for-command is evaluated once. Altering the value of the expression within the command-suite does not alter how often the command-suite is executed. A premature exit can be forced, however, by a terminating command.

The names of the naming of a for-command are 'bound-names', and may not be used outside of the command-suite to which they are bound. There is one exception to this rule: if a for-command is used in a test-refinement, and within the for-command a report-, succeed- or fail-command is executed, the currently bound names will temporarily survive as described under REFINED-TESTS (section 4.6.3).

See also: namings (4.5), quantifications (4.6.7).

4.4 EXPRESSIONS

An expression is evaluated to give a value. The evaluation of an expression cannot alter the contents of locations that currently exist, nor can it delete locations or create new locations that survive the expression. If an expression appears to alter a location, it effectively modifies a private 'scratchpad' *copy,* and the change is invisible outside the expression.

Expressions 123

---
expression:
- single-expression
- multiple-expression

---
single-expression:
- basic-expression
- (expression)

---
basic-expression:
- simple-expression
- formula$_{4.5}$

---
simple-expression:
- numeral$_{4.1}$
- address-inspection$_{4.2}$
- table-selection$_{4.3}$
- train-display$_{4.4}$
- refined-expression$_{4.6}$

---
tight-expression:
- simple-expression
- zeroadic-formula$_{4.5}$
- (expression)

Example basic-: simple-: tight-expressions:

```
   a         a         a
  -a
  a+b                (a+b)
```

The various kinds of expressions that are distinguished here serve to define the syntax in such a way that no parentheses are needed when the meaning is sufficiently clear.

If in a given context some name could be interpreted as a simple-expression — that is, as the name of a (shared or private) location, or of a refinement — and as a zeroadic formula — when it is the name of a zeroadic function — the interpretation as a simple-expression takes precedence.

For example, the command PI defined by

```
HOW TO PI:
    PUT 4 IN pi
    WRITE pi
```

outputs 4 and not 3.14159...

> multiple-expression:
> - single-expression , single-expression
> - single-expression , multiple-expression

Example multiple-expressions:

```
1, "abc"
(1, 0), (0, 1), (-1, 0), (0, -1)
```

The value of a multiple-expression composed of single-expressions separated by commas is the compound whose fields are the values of the successive single-expressions.

4.4.1 Numerals

> numeral:
> - fixed-notation optional-exponent-part

> fixed-notation:
> - integral-part optional-fractional-part
> - integral-part .
> - fractional-part

> integral-part:
> - digit optional-integral-part

> digit:
> - *any of the following signs:* 0 1 2 3 4 5 6 7 8 9

> fractional-part:
> - . digit
> - fractional-part digit

> exponent-part:
> - e optional-plus-or-minus integral-part

> plus-or-minus:
> - +
> - −

Example numerals

```
666
3.14
2.99793e8
2.99793e+8
1e-9
```

The value of a numeral is an exact number. For example, `1.25` stands for the exact number 5/4. The exponent-part, if present, gives the power of ten with which the value of the fixed-notation has to be multiplied. For example, `1.2345e2` has the same value as `1.2345*10**2`, which is the same number as `123.45`.

There are no notations for negative or approximate constants. However, the formula `-1.2345e2` may take the role of a 'negative constant', and, likewise, the formula `~1.2345e2` serves as an 'approximate constant'.

4.4.2 Address inspections

---
address-inspection:
- $name_{1.3}$

The value of an address-inspection is the value last put in the location created for the name which is the address-inspection. The location must already exist and hold a value.

4.4.3 Table selections

Table-selections are used to obtain an item from a table.

---
table-selection:
- $tight\text{-}expression_4$ [$expression_4$]

Example table-selections:

```
t[i, j]
{["yes"]: 1; ["no"]: 0}[answer]
```

The value of the tight-expression must be a table T, and the value of the expression between the square brackets must be a key K of T. The value of the table-selection is then the item of the table entry in T whose key is K.

4.4.4 Train displays

Train-displays are used to express values for trains.

---
train-display:
- text-display
- list-display
- table-display

Text displays

---
text-display:
- ′ optional-text-body ′
- ″ optional-text-body ″

The text-displays ′′ and ″″ stand for the empty text.

---
text-body:
- printable-character$_{1,1}$ optional-text-body
- conversion optional-text-body

In a text-display in the ′...′ style, any single quote ′ in the text must be written twice to give ′′. Otherwise, it would signal the end of the text-display. Similarly, in a text-display in the ″...″ style, any double quote ″ in the text must be written twice to give ″″. Finally, in either style of text-display, the back-quote ` must also be written twice, giving ``. Otherwise, it signals a conversion.

The quotes and conversion-signs that have to be written twice according to these rules correspond to one character of the resulting text. For example, the number of characters in ′x′′y″″z′ is 6, because it consists of one x, *one* ′ character, one y, *two* ″ characters, and finally one z. Another way to specify the same text is ″x′y″″″″z″.

---
conversion:
- ` expression$_4$ `

The requirement that some signs be written twice does not hold *inside* a conversion. For example, ′`t[′a′]`′ is proper, whereas ′`t[′′a′′]`′ is not.

Example text-displays:

```
′′
′He said: ″Don′′t!″′
″He said: ″″Don′t!″″″
′altitude is `a/1e3` km′
```

Expressions

The value of a text-display is the text composed of the characters given between the enclosing text quotes. If the text-display contains conversions, the expressions of these conversions are evaluated first and converted to a text in the same way as for a write-command. For example, since

```
WRITE 239*4649
```

causes the text 1 1 1 1 1 1 1 to be written, the text-display

```
"239 times 4649 gives `239*4649`"
```

is equivalent to

```
"239 times 4649 gives 1111111".
```

List displays

---
list-display:
- { optional-list-filler-series }

---
list-filler-series:
- list-filler
- list-filler ; list-filler-series

---
list-filler:
- single-expression$_4$
- single-expression$_4$ . . single-expression$_4$

The ambiguity in, e.g., {1...9}, is resolved by interpreting it as {1. .. 9}.

Example list-displays:

```
{ }
{x1; x2; x3}
{1..n-1}
{"a".."z"; "0".."9"; "."; """; '''}
```

The value of { } is an empty list. (It may also be an empty table; see below.)

The value of a list-display containing list-fillers is the list whose items are the values of those list-fillers. If values occur multiply, they give rise to multiple items in the list.

For a list-filler of the form $p..q$, p and q must both be integers, or both be characters (texts of length one). The values of the list-filler are then all integers or characters x such that $p \leq x \leq q$. For example,

```
{1..4} = {1; 2; 3; 4} and
{"A".."C"; ": OK"} = {"A"; "B"; "C"; ": OK"}.
```

128 *Description of ABC*

If $p > q$, the list-filler has no values. For example, {5; 7..4} = {5}.

Note that the expressions in a list-display need not be in the order of their values. For example, {3; 2; 1} is allowed and has the same value as {1..3}.

All items of a list must have the same type.

Table displays

---
table-display:
- { optional-table-filler-series }

---
table-filler-series:
- table-filler
- table-filler ; table-filler-series

---
table-filler:
- [expression$_4$] : single-expression$_4$

Example table-displays:
```
{}
{[i, j]: 0}
{[0]: {}; [1]: {0}}
{[name]: (month, day, year)}
```

The table-display {} stands for an empty table. Otherwise, each table-filler gives a table entry with key *K* and item *I*, where *K* is the value of the expression between square brackets, and *I* is the value of the single-expression following the colon. The result is then the table containing these table entries.

If there are *different* table entries with the same key, an error is reported. Multiple occurrences of the *same* table entry, however, are allowed. The extra occurrences are then simply discarded.

All keys of a table must have the same type. Similarly, all items must have the same type, but not necessarily the same type as the keys.

4.4.5 Formulas

---
formula:
- zeroadic-formula
- monadic-formula
- dyadic-formula

Expressions

zeroadic-formula:
- zeroadic-function

monadic-formula:
- monadic-function actual-operand

dyadic-formula:
- actual-operand dyadic-function actual-operand

zeroadic-function:
- name$_{1,3}$

monadic-function:
- *any one of* ~ + - */ /* # name$_{1,3}$

dyadic-function:
- *any one of* + - * / ** ^ ^^ | @ # << >< >> name$_{1,3}$

actual-operand:
- single-expression$_4$

The parsing ambiguities in these rules are resolved by priority rules, as follows:

1. If there is no parsing ambiguity (as in `1 + sin x`), or the order makes no difference (as in `a*b*c`, `a*b/c` or `a^b^c`), no parentheses are needed.
2. Functions have the following priorities, going from highest to lowest. Functions on the same line have equal priorities:

    ~ and monadic +
    monadic and dyadic #
    **
    monadic -
    * and /
    dyadic + and -
    @ and |
    ^^
    ^
    /* and */
    names
    <<, >< and >>.

3. All names (like `sin` or `floor`), and the functions `/*` and `*/`, may only be used having formulas as operands or in operands of higher-priority formulas if these operands are parenthesised (but not in, e.g., `exp abs x`, because of point 1 above, or in `5 round sin x >> 8` because of point 1 and `>>` having a lower priority).

Because of rule 1 both `a/b/c` and `a/b*c` are ambiguous. Because of rule 3 `sin x+y` is ambiguous. Each of these can be made correct by inserting parentheses, depending on the intention: either `(a/b)/c` or `a/(b/c)`, either `(a/b)*c` or `a/(b*c)`, and either `(sin x) + y` or `sin(x+y)`. Note that because of rule 3, `sin(x)+1` is just as wrong as `sin x + 1`.

The function `#` has been given a high priority, since expressions like `#t+1` are so common that it would be a nuisance to have to parenthesise these, and more so since `#(t+1)` is meaningless anyway. The reason for the high priority of the function `~` is to make `~0`, for example, for all practical purposes behave as a constant. The 'formatting' functions `<<`, `><` and `>>` have the lowest priority since they are practically always intended to operate on the whole preceding expression.

Example zeroadic-formula: monadic-formula: dyadic-formula:

    `pi`   `round(100*x)`   `2 round x`

Formulas with user-defined functions

A formula whose function is defined by a how-to is evaluated in the following steps:

1. A copy is made of the current environment (the value of all locations currently in use), and all computations during the evaluation of the formula take place in this 'scratchpad copy', which will be discarded once the evaluation is complete.
2. A modified copy of the how-to is made in which any private names in the how-to that might clash with names currently in use are systematically replaced by other names that do not cause conflict.
3. A location is created for each template-parameter of the modified how-to.
4. The value of each actual-operand is put in the location of the corresponding template-operand.
5. The command-suite of the modified how-to is executed.

The evaluation of the formula is complete when the execution of this command-suite terminates because of the execution of a return-command; the value of the formula is the value returned.

Note that in contrast to command-how-to's where results may be passed back to the parameters, one may safely use template-operands, and even shared names, in a function-how-to for intermediate computations.

Expressions 131

Formulas with predefined functions

A Functions on numbers

~x	returns an approximate number, as close as possible in arithmetic magnitude to x.
x+y	returns the sum of x and y. The result is exact if both operands are exact.
+x	returns the value of x.
x-y	returns the difference of x and y. The result is exact if both operands are exact.
-x	returns minus the value of x. The result is exact if the operand is exact.
x*y	returns the product of x and y. The result is exact if both operands are exact.
x/y	returns the quotient of x and y. The value of y must not be zero. The result is exact if both operands are exact.
x**y	returns x to the power y. The result is exact if x is exact and y is an integer. If x is negative, y must be an integer or an exact number with an odd denominator. If x is zero, y must not be negative. If y is zero, the result is one (exact or approximate depending on x).
n root x	returns (approximately) the n-th root of x. For example, 3 root x gives the cube root of x. If n is even, x must not be negative; n must not be zero.
root x	returns (approximately) the square root of x, the same as 2 root x. The value of x must not be negative.
abs x	returns the absolute value of x. The result is exact if the operand is exact.
sign x	returns -1 if x is negative, 0 if x is zero, and 1 otherwise.
floor x	returns the largest integer not exceeding x in arithmetic magnitude.
ceiling x	returns the smallest integer equal to or larger than x, the same as - floor -x.
n round x	returns x rounded to an exact number with n decimal places after the point, which is the same thing as

$$(\text{sign } x) * (10**-n) * \text{floor}((\text{abs } x)*10**n+.5).$$

For example, 4 round pi = 3.1416. The value of n must be an integer. It may be negative, and then the result will end with abs n zeros: (-2) round 666 = 700.

round x	returns x rounded to an integer, the same as 0 round x.
exactly x	returns the exact number equivalent to x, without any loss of precision. So, if x is an approximate number, ~exactly x is the same as x.
a mod n	returns the remainder after dividing a by n, which is the same as a-n*floor(a/n). Both operands may be approximate, and n may be negative, but not zero. The result is exact if both operands are exact.

/*x	returns a positive integer, the 'denominator' of x, that is, regarding x as the fraction p/q, with p and q reduced to smallest terms, q is returned. For example, /*(22/14) = 7. If x is zero, 1 is returned. The value of x must be an exact number.
*/x	returns the corresponding exact 'numerator' with the same sign as x, the same integer as (/*x)*x. So, if x is exact, x = (*/x)/(/*x). For example, */(22/14) = 11. The symbols */ and /* have been chosen to be suggestive of their purpose: if the number x is the fraction p/q, then */x returns p, and /*x returns q.
pi	returns approximately the number π, 3.14159265358979...
sin x	returns an approximate number by applying the sine function to x, with x in radians.
cos x	returns an approximate number by applying the cosine function to x, with x in radians.
tan x	returns an approximate number by applying the tangent function to x, the same as (sin x)/(cos x).
arctan x	returns an approximate number phi, in the range from (about) -pi/2 to +pi/2, such that x is approximated by tan phi.
radius z	z must be a compound of two numeric fields (x, y); the function returns (approximately) the distance in the Cartesian plane from the origin (0, 0) to the point (x, y), the same as root(x*x+y*y).
angle z	z must be a compound of two numeric fields (x, y); the function returns the angle in radians between the positive x-axis in the Cartesian plane and the line from the origin to (x, y). This is an approximate number in the range from (about) -pi to +pi. If both x and y are zero, an approximate zero is returned. The value of angle(1, y) is the same as that of arctan y. This diagram shows the relationship between angle and radius:

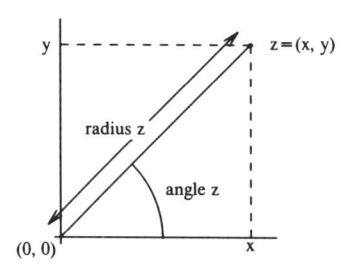

`c sin x`	these are all similar to their monadic counterparts, except that `x` and the result of `angle` are given in units where the circle is divided into `c` parts. For instance, in `360 sin x`, `x` is in degrees, and `(2*pi) sin x` is (approximately) the same as `sin x`. The value of `c` must not be zero.
`c cos x`	
`c tan x`	
`c arctan x`	
`c angle z`	
`e`	returns approximately the number e, 2.718281828459...
`exp x`	returns (approximately) the exponential function of `x`, the same as `e**x`.
`b log x`	returns (approximately) the logarithm with base `b` of `x`. For instance, the so-called 'common' logarithms have base 10, and so `10 log 2` returns approximately 0.30102999566398... The values of `b` and `x` must be positive.
`log x`	returns an approximate number by applying the natural logarithm function (with base e) to `x`, the same as `e log x`. The value of `x` must be positive. Thus, `b log x` is the same as `(log x)/(log b)`.
`random`	returns a random approximate number drawn from ~0 up to, but not including, ~1. The test `random < 0.25` will on the average succeed once in every four times it is performed.

B Functions on texts

`t^u`	returns the text consisting of `t` and `u` joined. For example, `"now"^"here" = "nowhere"`.
`t^^n`	returns the text consisting of `n` copies of `t` joined together. For example, `"Fi! "^^3 = "Fi! Fi! Fi! "`. The value of `n` must be an integer and not negative; if it is zero, the result is the empty text.
`t|n`	returns the initial part of `t` consisting of the first `n` characters. For example, `"scarface"|5 = "scarf"` and `"null"|0 = ""`. The value of `n` must be an integer and not negative; if `n` exceeds the length of `t`, then the whole text `t` is returned. For example, `"shorty"|99 = "shorty"`.
`t@n`	returns the final part of `t` obtained by deleting the first n−1 characters (and so starting at the n'th character). For example, `"lamplight"@4 = "plight"` and `"void"@5 = ""`. The value of `n` must be an integer and at most one more than the length of `t`. If `n` is less than 1, the whole text `t` is returned. For example, `"chunky"|#chunky-99 = "chunky"`.

Note that `\|` and `@` may be combined to select an arbitrary part of a text. For example, `"department"\|6@3 = "depart"@3 = "part"`. The same result may be obtained with `"department"@3\|4`. |
| `lower t` | returns the text `t` with all upper-case letters replaced by their lower-case equivalents. For example,

  `lower "The End" = "the end"`. |

134 *Description of ABC*

upper t   returns the text t with all lower-case letters replaced by their upper-case equivalents. For example,

        upper "The End" = "THE END".

stripped t   returns the text t with spaces stripped off from the beginning and end. For example,

        stripped "   The End   " = "The End".

split t   splits the text t into the parts separated by spaces, and returns a table whose keys are integers from 1 upwards, and whose items are the parts. For instance,

        split "   The End " = {[1]: "The"; [2]: "End"}
        split "" = {}.

C Function on tables

keys t   requires a table as operand, and returns a list of all keys in the table. For example, keys {[1]: 1; [4]: 2; [9]: 3} = {1; 4; 9}.

D Functions on trains

#t   returns the number of items in the train t (where duplicates in texts and lists are counted). For example,

        #"mississippi" = 11.

i#t   returns the number of items in t that are equal in value to i (which must be of the same type as the items of t). For example,

        "i"#"mississippi" = 4
        3#{1; 3; 3; 4} = 2
        3#{[1]: 3; [2]: 4; [3]: 3} = 2.

min t   returns the smallest item of t (for a text: first in the ASCII order, see section 4.1.1). For example

        min "uscule" = "c"
        min{1; 3; 3; 4} = 1
        min{[1]: 3; [2]: 4; [3]: 3} = 3.

The value of t must not be empty. To get the smallest (first) *key* of a table t, min keys t is used.

i min t   returns the smallest item in t *exceeding* the value of i (which must be of the same type as the items of t). For example

Expressions   135

```
"i" min "mississippi" = "m"
3 min {1; 3; 3; 4} = 4
3 min {[1]: 3; [2]: 4; [3]: 3} = 4.
```

There must be an item in t exceeding i.

max t and are like min, except that they return the largest item, and in the dyadic
i max t   case the largest item that is less in value than i. For example,
          `"m" max "mississippi" = "i"`.

t item n   returns the n-th item of t. The value of n must be an integer in the range
           {1..#t}.
           In fact, t item n, for a text t, is written as easily t@n|1. For
           a table, it is the same as t[(keys t) item n], which is something
           different from t[n], unless, of course, keys t = {1..#t}. For a list,
           t item 1 is min t.

choice t   returns an item chosen at random from t. In evaluating the formula
           choice {"Yes"; "Yes"; "I see"}, the item "Yes" is twice as
           likely to be chosen as the item "I see".

E Functions on values of all types

x<<n   returns x converted to a 'left-adjusted' text, that is, with space characters
        added to the right to make the length n. For example, 123<<6 =
        "123   ". In no case is the text truncated; if n is too small, the result-
        ing text is as long as necessary. The value of n must be an integer. See
        write-commands, section 4.3.4, for details about converting values to texts.

x><n   returns x converted to a 'centred' text, that is, with space characters ad-
        ded to both the left and the right, to make the length n. For example,
        123><6 = " 123 ". In no case is the text truncated. The value of n
        must be an integer.

x>>n   returns x converted to a 'right-adjusted' text, that is, with space characters
        added to the left to make the length n. For example, 123>>6 =
        "   123". In no case is the text truncated. The value of n must be an
        integer.

4.4.6 Refined expressions

refined-expression:
● name$_{1.3}$

The name of a refined-expression must occur as the name of one expression-refinement in
the how-to in which it occurs.

Example refined-expression:

```
stack.pointer
```

A refined-expression is evaluated in the following steps:

1. A copy is made of the current environment (the value of all locations currently in use), and all computations during the evaluation of the expression take place in this 'scratchpad copy', which will be discarded once the evaluation is complete.
2. The command-suite of the corresponding expression-refinement is executed.

The evaluation of the refined-expression is complete when the execution of this command-suite terminates because of the execution of a return-command; the value of the refined-expression is the value returned.

See also: expression-refinements (4.2.4).

4.5 ADDRESSES

An address is *located* to give a *location*, which may already exist, or be created to accommodate a value that is to be put in the location. A multiple-address refers to a multiple location, consisting of a combination of two or more single locations, called its components. A single location may hold arbitrarily complex values. Parts of text and table locations can be selected as locations of their own, in which values can be put without affecting the remainder of the text or table.

---
address:
- single-address
- multiple-address

---
single-address:
- basic-address
- (address)

---
basic-address:
- name$_{1.3}$
- text-selection-address$_{5.1}$
- table-selection-address$_{5.2}$

> multiple-address:
> - single-address , single-address
> - single-address , multiple-address

Example multiple-addresses:
```
nn, t2
(x0, y0), (x1, y1), (x2, y2), (x3, y3)
```

> naming:
> - single-naming
> - multiple-naming

> single-naming:
> - name$_{1.3}$
> - (naming)

> multiple-naming:
> - single-naming , single-naming
> - single-naming , multiple-naming

Namings are a restricted form of addresses; that is, all namings can be used as addresses, but the converse is not true. For example,

```
FOR a[1] IN {1..3}: WRITE a
```

is wrong, because a[1], although an address, is not a naming.

Example namings: single-namings:
```
a                        a
(a)                      (a)
(a, b, (c, d))  (a, b, (c, d))
a, b, (c, d)
```

A naming is located by locating it as if it were an address.

See also: put-commands (4.3.3).

4.5.1 Text-selection addresses

> text-selection-address:
> - address$_5$ | single-expression$_4$
> - address$_5$ @ single-expression$_4$

Example text-selection-addresses:

```
t|1
t@p
t|q@p
t@p+1
t@p|q-p+1
```

The address must hold a text T, and the value of the single-expression must be an integer N. If the sign used is |, then the text-selection-address indicates a location consisting of the first N characters of T, or, if N exceeds the length of T, consisting of the whole of T. N must be at least 0. A new text put in this location replaces these characters. For example, after

```
PUT "computer" IN tt
PUT "ne" IN tt|4
```

tt will contain the text "neuter".

If the sign used is @, then the text-selection-address indicates a location consisting of the characters of T starting with the N-th character, or, if N is less than 1, consisting of the whole of T. N must be at most one more than the length of T. A new text put in this location replaces these characters. For example, after

```
PUT "computer" IN tt
PUT "ass" IN tt@5
```

tt will contain the text "compass".

Note that the address itself may be a text-selection-address again. For example, after

```
PUT "computer" IN tt
PUT "m" IN tt@4|1
```

tt will contain the text "commuter".

Some special cases:
PUT "" IN t|1 removes the first character of the text in t; the same as PUT t@2 IN t.
PUT "." IN t@#t+1 appends a period to the text in t, the same as PUT t^"." IN t.

4.5.2 Table-selection addresses

---
table-selection-address:
- address$_5$ [expression$_4$]

Example table-selection-address:

    t[i, j]

The location of the address must hold a table. The value of the expression is a key K, to be used as selector. For each key in the table, there is a location for the corresponding item. If K is an existing key of the table, the location for the table-selection-address is that of the item corresponding to K. If a value I is then put in this location, the original item held in that location is superseded by I. If K is not an existing key and a value I is to be put in the table for this key, a new table entry consisting of K and I is inserted in the table. K must be of the same type as the other keys of the table, and I of the same type as the other table items.

4.6 TESTS

Tests are performed and do not return a value, but succeed or fail.
    Performing a test cannot alter the values of addresses that currently exist, nor can it create new addresses that survive the test, with the exception of the temporary survival of bound names as described under QUANTIFICATIONS (section 4.6.7) and REFINED-TESTS (section 4.6.3). If a test appears to alter a location, it effectively modifies a private, 'scratchpad' *copy,* and the change is invisible outside the test.

---
test:
- tight-test
- conjunction$_{6.4}$
- disjunction$_{6.5}$
- negation$_{6.6}$
- quantification$_{6.7}$

---
tight-test:
- (test)
- order-test$_{6.1}$
- examination$_{6.2}$
- refined-test$_{6.3}$

> right-test:
> - tight-test
> - negation$_{6.6}$
> - quantification$_{6.7}$

The various kinds of tests that are distinguished here serve to define the syntax in such a way that no parentheses are needed when the meaning is sufficiently clear.

4.6.1 Order tests

> order-test:
> - single-expression$_4$ order-sign single-expression$_4$
> - order-test order-sign single-expression$_4$

> order-sign:
> - *any one of* <   <=   =   <>   >=   >

(The order-sign <> stands for 'not equals'.)

Example order-tests:

```
(i', j') > (i, j)
"0" <= d <= "9"
fa <= f(x) >= fb
```

The single-expressions of an order-test must all have the same type. They are evaluated one by one, from left to right, and each adjacent pair is compared. As soon as a comparison does not comply with the given order-sign, the whole order-test fails and no further single-expressions are evaluated. The order-test succeeds if all comparisons comply with the specified order-signs.

An approximate number x is compared with an exact number e by applying the function `exactly` to x (see section 4.4.5A) and comparing the result with e.

Two exact numbers are equal if their numerical values are identical. Similarly two approximate numbers are equal if their numerical values are identical.

Two trains are equal if they have the same length, and their corresponding items, if any, are equal. Similarly, two compounds are equal if their corresponding fields are equal.

An exact number is smaller than another exact number if the numerical value of the first is smaller than that of the second. Similarly for two approximate numbers.

A train is smaller than another train if the first differing item in the first train is smaller than the corresponding item in the second train or if the length of the first train is smaller than that of the second, and all its items, if any, are equal to the corresponding items of the second.

Similarly, one compound is smaller than another if the first differing field of the first is smaller than its corresponding field in the second.

For instance, the following all succeed:

$$\text{\""} < \text{"a"} < \text{"ab"} < \text{"abc"} < \text{"abd"} < \text{"ac"} < \text{"b"}$$

4.6.2 Examinations

---
examination:
- zeroadic-examination
- monadic-examination
- dyadic-examination

---
zeroadic-examination:
- zeroadic-predicate

---
monadic-examination:
- monadic-predicate actual-operand$_{4.5}$

---
dyadic-examination:
- actual-operand$_{4.5}$ dyadic-predicate actual-operand$_{4.5}$

---
zeroadic-predicate:
- name$_{1.3}$

---
monadic-predicate:
- name$_{1.3}$

---
dyadic-predicate:
- name$_{1.3}$

Examinations with user-defined predicates

An examination whose predicate is defined by a how-to is performed as follows:

1. A copy is made of the current environment (the value of all locations currently in use), and all computations during the performing of the examination take place in this 'scratchpad copy', which will be discarded once the performing of the examination is complete.
2. A modified copy of the how-to is made in which any private names in the how-to that

might clash with names currently in use are systematically replaced by other names that do not cause conflict.
3. A location is created for each template-parameter of the modified how-to.
4. The value of each actual-operand is put in the location of the corresponding template-operand.
5. The command-suite of the modified how-to is executed.

The performing of the examination is complete when the execution of this command-suite terminates because of the execution of a report-, succeed- or fail-command; the examination succeeds or fails accordingly. Note that the operands of predicate- and function-how-to's are treated in exactly the same way.

Examinations with predefined predicates

`e in t`   accepts a train for the right operand. It succeeds if `e#t > 0` succeeds, that is, if the value `e` occurs in `t`.
`e not.in t` is the same as `(NOT e in t)`.
`exact n` accepts a number as operand. It succeeds if `n` is an exact number.

4.6.3 Refined tests

refined-test:
● name$_{1.3}$

Example refined-test:

```
special.case
```

A refined-test is performed in the following steps:

1. A copy is made of the current environment (the value of all locations currently in use), and all computations during the performing of the test take place in this 'scratchpad copy', which will be discarded once the performing of the test is complete.
2. The command-suite of the corresponding test-refinement is executed.

The performing of the refined-test is complete when the execution of this command-suite terminates because of the execution of a report-, succeed- or fail-command, and the refined-test succeeds or fails accordingly.

Any bound names set by a for-command or a quantification (see 4.6.7) at that time will temporarily survive for those parts that are reachable only by virtue of the outcome of the test. This is so that you can turn any test into a refined-test with the same effect.
For example, in

```
        IF divisible AND n > d**2: WRITE d
        ...
    divisible:
        REPORT SOME d IN {2..n-1} HAS n mod d = 0,
```
the bound name d is set to a divisor of n if the refined-test succeeds, and since the part n > d**2 is only reached after success, d may be used there. The same is true for the write-command using d. However, the line after (indicated with three dots) can be reached if the divisibility test fails, so there d has ceased to exist and may not be used.

See also: test-refinements (4.2.4).

4.6.4 Conjunctions

---
conjunction:
- tight-test$_6$ AND right-test$_6$
- tight-test$_6$ AND conjunction

Example conjunctions:
```
    a > 0 AND b > 0
    i in keys t AND t[i] in keys u AND u[t[i]] <> "dummy"
```
The tests of the conjunction, separated by AND, are performed one by one, from left to right. As soon as one of these tests fails, the whole conjunction fails and no further parts are performed. The conjunction succeeds if all its tests succeed.

4.6.5 Disjunctions

---
disjunction:
- tight-test$_6$ OR right-test$_6$
- tight-test$_6$ OR disjunction

Example disjunctions:
```
    a <= 0 OR b <= 0
    n = 0 OR s[1] = s[n] OR t[1] = t[n]
```
The tests of the disjunction, separated by OR, are performed one by one, from left to right. As soon as one of these tests succeeds, the whole disjunction succeeds and no further parts are performed. The disjunction fails if all its tests fail.

4.6.6 Negations

---
negation:
- NOT right-test$_6$

Example negation:

    NOT a subset b

A negation succeeds if its right-test fails, and fails if that test succeeds.

4.6.7 Quantifications

Quantifications are easy ways of finding out if a test is true for no items, or at least one, or every item of a train.

---
quantification:
- quantifier ranger$_{3.21}$ HAS right-test$_6$

---
quantifier:
- SOME
- EACH
- NO

Example quantifications:

    SOME i IN samples HAS NOT low <= i <= high
    EACH i, j IN keys t HAS t[i, j] = t[j, i]
    NO d IN {2..n-1} HAS n mod d = 0

The names of the naming of a quantification are 'bound names', and so may not be used outside the quantification except as described below.

The meaning of quantifications will first be described for the case of SOME. The value of the expression must be a train. One by one, each item of that train is put in the location of the naming, and each time the right-test is then performed. The quantification succeeds as soon as the right-test succeeds once. It fails only if the train is exhausted without the right-test ever succeeding (thus also if the train is empty).

If the quantification succeeds, the bound names set at that moment will temporarily survive and may be used in those parts that are reachable only by virtue of the outcome of the test.

For example, in

    IF (SOME d IN {2..n-1} HAS n mod d = 0) AND n > d**2:
        WRITE d

the bound name d is set to a divisor of n if the quantification succeeds, and since the part n > d**2 is only reached after success, d may be used there. The same is true for the write-command using d. So, if n has the value 77, 7 will be written, since the test n mod d = 0 succeeds the first time when d is set to 7 (and 77 > 7**2). However, the line after (indicated with three dots) can be reached if the divisibility test fails, so there d has ceased to exist and may not be used.

The meaning of a quantification SOME id IN train HAS prop can also be described as the meaning of the refined-test test.if.some, given a test-refinement

```
test.if.some:
    FOR id IN train:
        IF prop: SUCCEED
    FAIL
```

The meaning of EACH id IN train HAS prop is the same as that of NOT SOME id IN train HAS NOT prop. In other words, an EACH quantification succeeds only if its right-test succeeds each time, or the train is empty.

The meaning of NO id IN train HAS prop is the same as that of NOT SOME id IN train HAS prop. In other words, a NO quantification succeeds only if its right-test fails each time, or the train is empty.

The rules for temporary survival follow from those for SOME. So an EACH or NO quantification will only have set its bound names on failure. Thus, in the following, the bound name d survives into the ELSE:

```
SELECT:
    NO d IN {2..n-1} HAS n mod d = 0: WRITE "prime"
    ELSE: WRITE "divisible by `d`"
```

See also: for-commands (4.3.21).

APPENDIX A

ABC Quick Reference

COMMANDS

WRITE *expr*	Write to screen; / before or after *expr* gives new line
READ *address* EG *expr*	Read expression from terminal to *address*; *expr* is example of type to be read.
READ *address* RAW	Read line of text
PUT *expr* IN *address*	Put value of *expr* in *address*
SET RANDOM *expr*	Start random sequence for `random` and `choice`
REMOVE *expr* FROM *list*	Remove one element from *list*
INSERT *expr* IN *list*	Insert in right place
DELETE *address*	Delete location or table entry
PASS	Do nothing
KEYWORD expr KEYWORD ...	Execute user-defined command
KEYWORD	Execute refined command
CHECK *test*	Check *test* and stop if it fails

IF *test*:
    commands
	If *test* succeeds, execute *commands*;
	    no ELSE allowed

SELECT:
    test: *commands*
    ...
    test: *commands*
	Select one alternative:
	    try each *test* in order
	    (one must succeed;
	    the last *test* may be ELSE)

WHILE *test*:
    commands
	As long as *test* succeeds,
	    execute *commands*

FOR *name*,... IN *train*: *commands*	Take each element of *train* in turn

HOW-TO's

HOW TO *KEYWORD*... *commands*	Defines new command *KEYWORD* ...
HOW TO RETURN f: *commands*	Defines new function f with no arguments (returns a value)
HOW TO RETURN $f\,x$: *commands*	Defines new function f with one argument
HOW TO RETURN $x\,f\,y$: *commands*	Defines new function f with two arguments

HOW TO REPORT *pr*: *commands*   Defines new predicate *pr* with no arguments (succeeds/fails)
HOW TO REPORT *pr x*: *commands*   Defines new predicate *pr* with one argument
HOW TO REPORT *x pr y*: *commands*   Defines new predicate *pr* with two arguments
SHARE *name*, ...   (Before commands of how-to) share names

Refinements (after the commands of a how-to)

KEYWORD : *commands*   Defines command-refinement
name: *commands*   Defines expression- or test-refinement

Terminating commands

QUIT   Leave command-how-to or command-refinement, or leave ABC
RETURN *expr*   Leave function-how-to or expression-refinement, return value of *expr*
REPORT *test*   Leave predicate-how-to or test-refinement, report outcome of *test*
SUCCEED   The same, report success
FAIL   The same, report failure

EXPRESSIONS AND ADDRESSES

666, 3.14, 3.14e-9   Exact constants
expr, *expr*, ...   Compound
name, *name*, ...   Naming (may also be used as address)
text @ *p*   "ABCD"@2 = "BCD" (also address)
text | *q*   "ABCD"|3 = "ABC" (also address)
text @ *p* | *q*   "ABCD"@2|1 = "BCD"|1 = "B"
table [*expr*]   Table selection (also address)
"Jan", 'Feb', 'Won''t!'   Textual displays (empty: "" or '')
"value = `*expr*`;"   Conversion of *expr* to text
{1; 2; 2; ...}   List display (empty: {})
{1..9; ...}, {"a".."z"; ...}   List of consecutive values
{["Jan"]: 1; ["Feb"]: 2; ...}   Table display (empty: {})
f, *f x*, *x f y*   Result of function *f* (no permanent effects)
name   Result of refinement (no permanent effects)

ABC Quick Reference 149

TESTS

$x < y$, $x <= y$, $x >= y$, $x > y$	Order tests
$x = y$, $x <> y$	(`<>` means 'not equals')
$0 <= d < 10$	
pr, *pr x*, *x pr y*	Outcome of predicate *pr* (no permanent effects)
name	Outcome of refinement (no permanent effects)
test AND *test* AND ...	Fails as soon as one of the tests fails
test OR *test* OR ...	Succeeds as soon as one of the tests succeeds
NOT *test*	
SOME *name*,... IN *train* HAS *test*	Sets *name*, ... on success
EACH *name*,... IN *train* HAS *test*	Sets *name*, ... on failure
NO *name*,... IN *train* HAS *test*	Sets *name*, ... on failure

PREDEFINED FUNCTIONS AND PREDICATES

Functions and predicates on numbers

`~x`	Approximate value of x
`exactly x`	Exact value of x
`exact x`	Test if x is exact
`+x, x+y, x-y, -x, x*y, x/y`	Plain arithmetic
`x**y`	x raised to the power y
`root x, n root x`	Square root, n-th root
`abs x, sign x`	Absolute value, sign ($= -1, 0,$ or $+1$)
`round x, floor x, ceiling x`	Rounded to whole number
`n round x`	x rounded to n digits after decimal point
`a mod n`	Remainder of a on division by n
`*/x`	Numerator of exact number x
`/*x`	Denominator
`random`	Random approximate number r, $0 \leq r < 1$
`e, exp x`	Base of natural logarithms, exponential function
`log x, b log x`	Natural logarithm, logarithm to the base b
`pi, sin x, cos x, tan x, arctan x`	Trigonometric functions, with x in radians
`angle (x, y), radius (x, y)`	Angle of and radius to point (x, y)
`c sin x, c cos x, c tan x`	Similar, with the circle divided into c parts
`c arctan x, c angle (x, y)`	(e.g. 360 for degrees)

Functions on texts

t^*u*	*t* and *u* joined into one text
t^^*n*	*t* repeated *n* times
lower *t*	lower "aBc" = "abc"
upper *t*	upper "aBc" = "ABC"
stripped *t*	*t* with leading and trailing spaces removed
split *t*	*t* split into words

Function on tables

keys *table*	List of all keys in *table*

Functions and predicates on trains

#*train*	Number of elements in *train*
e#*train*	Number of elements equal to *e*
e in *train*, *e* not.in *train*	Test for presence or absence
min *train*	Smallest element of *train*
e min *train*	Smallest element larger than *e*
max *train*, *e* max *train*	Largest element
train item *n*	*n*-th element
choice *train*	Random element

Functions on all types

x<<*n*	*x* converted to text, aligned left in width *n*
x><*n*	The same, centred
x>>*n*	The same, aligned right

THE CHARACTERS

```
 !"#$%&'()*+,-./
0123456789:;<=>?
@ABCDEFGHIJKLMNO
PQRSTUVWXYZ[\]^_
`abcdefghijklmno
pqrstuvwxyz{|}~
```

This is the order of all characters that may occur in a text.
(The first is a space.)

APPENDIX B

Differences between ABC and B

ABC is a result of several years development. The earlier versions of the language were known by the name *B* (no relation to the predecessor of C). For the benefit of readers who know and used *B*, here is a short summary of the major differences between the languages. Only an overview is given here: see the main body of the book for more details.

Representations

Names may now include points, such as `number.of.occurrences`.
 The exponent part of a number is now written with a lower-case e rather than upper-case: `1e-10`. Furthermore, numbers with exponent parts are exact and not approximate numbers.

How-to's

The keyword `HOW'TO` is now two keywords `HOW TO`. Furthermore, the keywords `YIELD` and `TEST` have been replaced by `HOW TO RETURN` and `HOW TO REPORT` respectively.
 All keywords up to the first parameter of a command are now significant, rather than just the first keyword.
 Parameter passing has changed for command how-to's: any value that the parameter has is copied into the template parameter when the command is invoked, and if the value has changed at the end, it is copied back.
 Template parameters to commands may now be multiple names, such as

```
HOW TO MOVE x, y TO a, b:
```

Predefined commands

The keyword `SET'RANDOM` has become two keywords `SET RANDOM`.
 `CHOOSE` has been replaced by a function `choice`. Similarly, `DRAW` has been replaced by `random`.
 There is a new command `PASS`.

Expressions

Range displays for lists may now contain more than one range, such as {"a".."z"; "0".."9"}.

In a range-display, if the lower-bound is greater than the upper-bound, the range is empty, rather than giving an error.

The priorities of some operators have been changed. In particular, @ and | have been integrated into the priorities of operators.

The expressions "word"|8 and "word"@-8 both return "word" now, rather than failing.

Predefined functions

There are four new functions on texts: lower, upper, split, and stripped.

There are three new functions on numbers: angle, radius, and exactly. The numeric function atan has been renamed arctan. Dyadic versions of sin, cos, tan, and arctan have been added.

The function n th'of t has been renamed and changed to t item n.

As mentioned above, choice and random have replaced CHOOSE and DRAW.

Tests

The test 1 = ~1 now succeeds. A new predefined predicate exact has been introduced to test if a number is exact or approximate. The predicate not'in is now spelt not.in.

PARSING has been completely removed.

Terminology

Several terms have been renamed. A unit is now called a *how-to*, a target is now called an *address*. Formal parameters are now called *template parameters*. Texts, lists and tables are collectively called *trains*. A tag is now a *name*. An identifier is a *naming*.

APPENDIX C

ABC Implementations

We have tried to make the behaviour of all ABC implementations as identical as possible. Therefore, this appendix is only about machine particularities such as what files are involved, where they are kept, and so on. With all implementations, you should first check if there is a file README on the disk or tape, and if so read it: it will be an update on the documentation.

Workspaces

When you run ABC for the first time, it creates a directory (or folder) called abc where it makes separate directories for each workspace you make. This directory is created in your home directory on Unix, in the folder where ABC was started from on the Macintosh, and in the root directory of the current disk on other implementations. Additionally, in directory abc, it creates a file wsgroup.abc which maps workspace names to directory names, and gives the remembered name of the last workspace used.

In each workspace directory, the system creates files ending with the following names:

.cmd for commands
.zfd for zeroadic functions
.mfd for monadic functions
.dfd for dyadic functions
.zpd for zeroadic predicates
.mpd for monadic predicates
.dpd for dyadic predicates
.cts for permanent location contents.

Additionally it makes the following in each workspace:

perm.abc	mapping ABC names to file names
position.abc	position when a file last visited
suggestion.abc	suggestions for this workspace.

Error messages

All implementations, except on the Macintosh, use a file abc.msg which contains nearly all error messages produced by ABC. You can translate this file, to produce a foreign-language version of the error messages. Messages marked with an asterisk '*' are system errors, and in principle shouldn't occur, so do not need to be translated. ABC looks for this file in a number of places: in the directory where you started ABC up, in the workspaces directory mentioned above, or in one of the directories in the PATH environment variable, if set. In other words, put the messages file in the same directory as the ABC program itself, or in the workspaces directory.

On the Macintosh, the errors are resources which you must edit with a resource editor.

Key bindings

ABC comes with a standard set of 'key-bindings' (which keys are used for which operation) to suit the keyboard of the machine you are using. To see these defaults, type ? at the command prompt >>>. You can change these bindings by running the program abckeys (though not on the Macintosh). This program is self-documenting, and allows you to specify your own bindings for the operations described in the chapter on using ABC. For any operation you may specify as many alternatives as you wish. If a new binding clashes with another binding, the old binding is removed.

The program then writes a file in the abc directory mentioned above, specifying the bindings. This file is then read on start-up by the ABC system.

This file is called abc.key, except on Unix, where you may have one such file for each terminal type you use. There, each file is called abckeys_*term*, where *term* is the contents of the Unix environment variable TERM.

There are three special entries that you can define. The entry ignore is for any sequence you want the system to ignore (this is mainly useful for using the ABC system using a modem on a noisy telephone line). The entry term-init specifies characters that are sent to the screen when ABC is started; you can use this to send characters to set the screen background colour for instance, or to set programmable function keys, if your terminal has them. Similarly, term-done specifies what is to be sent when ABC finishes.

Running ABC

Apart from running ABC as described in the chapter on using ABC, there are a number of optional flags that you can give when starting ABC up.

Workspace options

Starting ABC up with

    `abc -w name`

starts in workspace `name`, instead of the default (which is whichever you were in last time, or in workspace `first`, if this is the first time).
    Starting with

    `abc -W dir`

uses the group of workspaces in `dir` instead of the `abc` directory mentioned above. You can combine it with the `-w` option, for example:

    `abc -W c:\programs -w demo`

Finally,

    `abc -w path`

uses `path` as the current workspace (in which case no `-W` option is allowed). For instance,

    `abc -w c:\programs\demo`

The difference between this, and the example above, is that the system doesn't use `c:\programs` as a repository for other workspaces, and doesn't make the `wsgroup.abc` file, so you can't change workspace from within ABC using this form.

Special tasks

There are a few special options for dealing with workspaces from outside ABC.

    `abc -i tab`

fills table `tab` with text lines from standard input. Use the `-w` option to be sure of which workspace it will be put in. For instance, on Unix and MS-DOS,

    `abc -w demo -i text < readme`

will convert the file `readme` in the current directory into an ABC table called `text` in workspace `demo`.
    Similarly

    `abc -o tab`

writes such a table out to standard output. For instance

    `abc -w demo -o text > newfile`

The command

    abc -l

lists the how-to's in a workspace on standard output; you can then send this output to the printer. Use the -w option to be sure of which workspace will be listed. For instance, on MS-DOS:

    abc -l -w demo > prn:

Finally, there are two options to restore the ABC internal files, if they have been accidentally lost, or if you have added some how-to's to a workspace independently of the ABC system:

    abc -r

recovers a workspace when its index is lost, for instance

    abc -w demo -r

and

    abc -R

recovers the index of a group of workspaces.

Running non-interactively

You can give the names of files containing ABC commands to ABC, and then it runs the commands instead of starting up interactively. Input for READ commands then comes from the standard input. For instance, if the file run contains

    WRITE 2+2

then the command

    abc run

will cause 4 to be written. Similarly, if run contains

    DEMO1

then the command

    abc -w demo run

will run the command DEMO1 from the workspace demo, and then stop.

The Atari ST implementation

There are four files supplied: the program `abc.tos` itself, the help file `abc.hlp`, the error message file `abc.msg`, and the program `abckeys.tos` for changing your key bindings. When running ABC, you may use the mouse as described in the chapter on using ABC.

If you start ABC up from the desktop, and you want to use the options given above, like `-w`, you should rename `abc.tos` to `abc.ttp`. There is an additional facility for redirecting input and output: the parameter `>outfile` redirects all output from ABC to the file called `outfile`, and similarly `<infile` takes its input from the file called `infile` (you can call the files anything you want).

There is a bug in some versions of the Atari desktop that converts all lower-case letters to upper-case when you give the options. This means that you can't use the options `-w` and `-r` (because the program sees them as `-W` and `-R`). If you have this bug and you want to use these two options, use the letters `-x` and `-s` instead (the next letters in the alphabet after W and R).

The IBM PC implementation

There are four files supplied: the program `abc.exe` itself, the help file `abc.hlp`, the error message file `abc.msg`, and the program `abckeys.exe` for changing your key bindings.

If your screen size is non-standard, or your machine is not 100% BIOS compatible (which is unusual these days), you can specify the screen-size, and whether to use the BIOS or ANSI.SYS for output, by typing after the `A>` prompt, before you start ABC up, one of the following:

    SET SCREEN=ANSI lines cols
    SET SCREEN=BIOS lines cols

If you are going to use `ANSI.SYS`, be sure you have the line

    DEVICE=ANSI.SYS

in your `CONFIG.SYS` file. Consult the DOS manual for further details.

The Macintosh implementation

There are three files supplied: the program `MacABC` itself, the help file `MacABC.help`, and `MacABC.doc`, a MacWrite document containing a version of the help file. The help file should be in the same folder as MacABC, or in your system folder. To change the error messages, you must use a resource editor.

158   *ABC Implementations*

ABC runs in a single window. You'll notice that most operations, as well as being possible from the keyboard, are also menu entries. You can start ABC up by double-clicking the `MacABC` icon in which case you start up in the last workspace used, or by double-clicking on any icon in a workspace, in which case you start up in that workspace. In this latter case, if the filename of the icon you clicked on ends in `.cmd`, that how-to is executed, but the how-to must not have any parameters.

Instead of the special option flags mentioned above, most of the tasks, like recovering a workspace, can be done from the File menu.

The Unix implementation

If the system has been set up right, you should be able to say `man abc` to get online documentation about ABC.

There is an additional option when running ABC:

`abc -e`

uses the editor named in the Unix EDITOR environment variable as editor to edit how-to's.

Apart from the `abckeys_*` files mentioned above, ABC gets some of its information about the terminal from `termcap` (in particular whether there are arrow keys, and whether there are function keys), and some information from the `stty` settings (in particular what your interrupt character is; see the manual for `stty` if you want to change it).

If your version of Unix supports job control, you can suspend ABC in the normal way (usually using control-Z).

Finally, if your terminal has a mouse, ABC can support it if there is a way for the mouse to send a click and its position as a sequence of characters.

To configure ABC to be able to do this, use `abckeys` to set the (goto) operation to the characters that get sent when a click occurs, and add two extra fields to your termcap entry to specify how the system finds out where the click occurred: `sp` which gives the characters that have to be sent to enquire where the click occurred, and `cp` which says what the reply looks like. These are both in the same format as other cursor-addressing strings in termcap — see the termcap manual for more information.

If the mouse click sends the position as well, you must set the (goto) operation to the initial characters that get sent (minus the position) and set `sp` to the empty string.

As an example of one of the more popular interfaces, in an *xterm* window, if you set your ABC *term-init* (using `abckeys`) to send the characters "ESC [?9h", mouse-clicks will then send their position as "ESC [M*xy*", where *x* and *y* are two characters specifying the position. So, specify that the binding for the (goto) operation (still using `abckeys`) is "ESC [M", and add the following two fields to your termcap entry: `sp=:cp=%r%+!%+!` (`sp` is empty because a mouse click sends the position).

You should set `term-done` in `abckeys` to "ESC [?9l" so that mouse clicks return to their normal behaviour when you leave ABC.

Index

", 102, 126
#, 3, 5, 6, 23, 129, 134
', 102, 126
(, 123, 136, 137, 139
), 123, 136, 137, 139
**, 129, 131
*, 129, 131
*/, 3, 129, 132
+, 124, 129, 131
,, 111, 124, 137
-, 124, 129, 131
.., 127
., 102, 124
/*, 3, 129, 132
/, 2, 17, 111, 129, 131
:, 76, 77, 104, 105, 107, 119, 120, 121, 128
::, 76, 77, 78
;, 127, 128
<, 140
<<, 17, 129, 135
<=, 140
<>, 140
=, 89, 140
==, 67
>, 88, 140
><, 129, 135
>=, 140
>>, 88, 129, 135
>>>, 63
?, 63, 154
@, 3, 129, 133, 138
[, 125, 128, 139
\, 1, 101
], 125, 128, 139
^, 3, 17, 129, 133

^^, 3, 129, 133
`, 13, 18, 126
{, 127, 128
|, 3, 17, 129, 133, 138
}, 127, 128
~, 129, 131

abckeys program, 154
abs, 3, 131
absolute value, 3
accept, 64, 65, 66, 67, 69, 70, 72, 75, 86
accuracy of floating point, 40
actual-operand, **129**, 141
actual-parameter, **117**
address, 1, 109, 110, 113, 114, 117, 121, 128, **136**, 137, 138, 139
address-inspection, 123, **125**
address position, 118
alternative, 10
alternative-sequence, **120**
alternative-suite, **120**
ambiguity, 126, 128
AND, 12, 70, 143
angle, 132
approximate constant, 125
approximate number, 2, 39, 97, 140
arctan, 132
arrays, xii, 6
Atari ST, xiii, 157

back-quote, 126
bags, 28
basic-address, **136**

159

160   *Index*

basic-expression, **123**
bound names, 116, 117, 121, 122, 139, 142, 144
braces, 65
brackets, 65, 87

capital letters, 69, 70, 102
`ceiling`, 2, 131
centred text, 135
changing how-to's, 76, 77
changing the contents of locations, 89
character, 97, 98, 126
CHECK, 68, 110
check-command, 108, **110**
`choice`, 11, 21, 135
closure, 36
collective-noun, 99
command, **108**, 109
command definition, 1
command-how-to, 7, 103, **104**, 115, 117
command prompt, 63, 64
command-refinement, **107**, 115, 119
command-sequence, **109**
command-suite, 103, 107, **108**, 119, 120, 121
command-template, **104**
comment, 1, **101**
comment-body, **101**, 102
compound, 1, 4, 97, 122, 136
conjunction, 139, **143**
connective, 99
continued fractions, 41
control-command, 2, 8, 10, **108**
conversion, **126**
convert a character to a number, 33
convert to a text, 18, 111, 126, 128
converting between exact and approximate numbers, 2
(copy), 85, 89
copy buffer, 85, 86
copying between how-to's, 86
copying between workspaces, 88, 89

`cos`, 132
cross-referencer, 52

declaration, 10, 13
declarative, 99
decrease-indentation, 101, 109, 120
degrees, 3
DELETE, 6, 67, 114
(delete), 71, 77, 78, 79
delete to copy buffer, 86
delete-command, 108, **114**
deleting brackets and quotes, 87
deleting how-to's, 78
deleting permanent locations, 67
deleting workspaces, 88
denominator, 3, 128, 132
derivative of a polynomial, 43
difference of two polynomials, 42
digit, 102, **124**
disjunction, 139, **143**
document formatter, 49
(down), 78, 84
(downline), 71
dyadic, 8, 27, 104, 105
dyadic-examination, **141**
dyadic-examination-template, **106**
dyadic-formula, 128, **129**
dyadic-formula-template, **105**
dyadic-function, **129**
dyadic-predicate, **141**

e, 124, 133
EACH, 12, 70, 144
editing, 76, 77
editing values, 89
editor, xii
EDITOR environment variable, 158
efficiency, 27
EG, 112
Eliza, 46, 60
ELSE, 10, 70, 121

Index

else-alternative, **120**
empty, **101**
empty list, 126
empty table, 126
environment, xii
equality, definition of, 140
error messages, 65, 77, 90, 154
evaluate a polynomial, 44
`exact`, 142
exact number, 2, 97, 140
`exactly`, 131
examination, 105, 139, **141**
examination-template, **105**
`exit`, 64, 72, 76, 77, 78, 89
`exp`, 3, 133
exponent-part, **124**
exponential function, 3
expression, 1, 110, 113, 115, 117, 122, **123**, 125, 126, 128, 139
expression position, 118
expression-refinement, **107**, 109, 115, 135
`extend`, 78, 80

FAIL, 12, 68, 117
fail-command, 108, 109, **117**, 141, 142
field, 97, 98
files, xi, 153, 155, 156, 157
finishing a session, 67
`first`, 88
`first`, 78, 79, 82
`first` workspace, 155
fixed-notation, **124**
floating point, 2
`floor`, 2, 131
focus, 63, 71, 79, 80, 82, 84, 85
focus move, 78, 82, 84
focus operations summary, 95
FOR, 2, 3, 4, 5, 6, 68, 121
for-command, 108, **121**
formatter, 49
formatting functions, 130

formula, 104, 123, **128**
formula-template, **104**
fractional-part, **124**
FROM, 113
function call, 128
function-how-to, 8, 103, **104**, 109, 115, 128
functions, typing, 73

garbage-collection, 34
generate sentences, 55, 57
global, 103
`goto`, 158
grammar, 57
graphs, 33
guessing game, 21

HAS, 144
`help`, 63
hole, 63, 67, 71, 72, 77, 85, 86
HOW TO, 8, 72, 104
how-to, 1, 76, 88, **103**
HOW TO ADD, 24
HOW TO ADD HELP FOR, 25
HOW TO ADD NODE, 31
HOW TO ADD TO, 16, 20
HOW TO APPEND, 25
HOW TO APPEND WORD, 56
HOW TO CALCULATE ACCURACY, 40
HOW TO DISPLAY, 25
HOW TO DISPLAY GRAMMAR, 57
HOW TO DISPLAY TREE, 31
HOW TO EMPTY, 23
HOW TO EXPRESSION, 32
HOW TO FORMAT, 49
HOW TO GENERATE, 58
HOW TO GENERATE IMITATION FROM, 55
HOW TO GUESS, 21
HOW TO HELP, 25, 26
HOW TO IMITATE, 55
HOW TO INCLUDE, 28

HOW TO INPUT, 58
HOW TO LIST, 26, 27
HOW TO OPERAND, 32
HOW TO ORACLE, 46
HOW TO OUTPUT, 53
HOW TO PI, 41
HOW TO PLAY, 22
HOW TO POP, 24
HOW TO PRINT POLY, 43
HOW TO PRINT TEL, 17, 18
HOW TO PROMPT, 58
HOW TO PUSH, 23
HOW TO REPORT, 12, 74, 105
HOW TO RETURN, 8, 73, 104
HOW TO RETURN analysed, 55
HOW TO RETURN at, 44
HOW TO RETURN closure, 36
HOW TO RETURN common.with, 28
HOW TO RETURN compiled, 31
HOW TO RETURN constant, 44
HOW TO RETURN derivative, 43
HOW TO RETURN filled, 52
HOW TO RETURN formatted, 51
HOW TO RETURN generated, 60
HOW TO RETURN index, 52, 53
HOW TO RETURN integral, 44
HOW TO RETURN inverse, 17, 19, 20
HOW TO RETURN less, 28
HOW TO RETURN listed, 27
HOW TO RETURN minus, 42
HOW TO RETURN next.char, 32
HOW TO RETURN normalised, 42
HOW TO RETURN plus, 42
HOW TO RETURN popped, 24
HOW TO RETURN power, 42
HOW TO RETURN powerset, 29
HOW TO RETURN primes, 38
HOW TO RETURN prod, 35
HOW TO RETURN reachable.from, 34, 35
HOW TO RETURN rep, 39

HOW TO RETURN reply, 48
HOW TO RETURN set, 29
HOW TO RETURN times, 38, 42
HOW TO RETURN top, 23
HOW TO RETURN value, 33
HOW TO RETURN with, 28
HOW TO RETURN zero, 44
HOW TO SAVE, 19
how-to-script, **103**, 104, 105
HOW TO SESSION, 60
HOW TO SHOW, 34
HOW TO SIEVE TO, 37
HOW TO SIMULATE, 30
HOW TO SKIP CHAR, 32
HOW TO TAKE, 30
HOW TO TALK WITH ELIZA, 48
HOW TO TERM, 32
HOW TO TRY, 22
HOW TO UPDATE, 55

IBM PC, xiii, 157
IF, 119
if-command, 108, **119**
imitation, 55
immediate command, 9, 15, 66, 68, 108
immediate-command, 115
implementations, xiii, 153
IN, 110, 113, 122
in, 11, 142
incompatible types, 90
incomplete how-to's, 78
increase-indentation, 101, 109, 120
indent, 101
indentation, xii, 2, 69, 72, 101
input, 13, 15, 155
input-format, **112**
INSERT, 5, 113
insert-command, 108, **113**
integer, 97, 126, 128
integral of a polynomial, 43
integral-part, **124**
⟨interrupt⟩, 64, 68

Index

interrupt, 30, 108, 158
`inverse`, 54
inverse of a graph, 35
`item`, 3, 5, 6, 135
item, 4, 6, 7, 97, 98, 99, 144

key, 6, 97, 99, 125, 126, 128, 139
key-bindings, 63, 154
`keys`, 6, 16, 134
keyword, 70, 101, **102**, 103, 106, 117, 119
keyword-suite, **102**, 104, 107, 117, 119

large how-to's, 77
⸨last⸩, 78, 79
⸨left⸩, 78, 84, 86
left adjusted text, 135
list, 2, 4, 21, 97
list-display, 126, **127**
list-filler, **127**
list-filler-series, **127**
list item, 113
local, 103
location, 1, 4, 9, 67, 89, 103, 110, 114, 136, 137, 139
`log`, 3, 133
logarithm, 3
⸨look⸩, 70
`lower`, 47, 133
lower-case letter, 102

Macintosh, xiii, 157
macintosh, 154
`max`, 5, 6, 135
messages file, 154
`min`, 5, 6, 134
mod, 3, 39, 131
monadic, 8, 27, 104, 105
monadic-examination, **141**
monadic-examination-template, **106**

monadic-formula, 128, **129**
monadic-formula-template, **105**
monadic-function, **129**
monadic-predicate, **141**
mouse, 84, 157, 158
moving text, 85
moving the focus, 71
moving things between workspaces, 89
multi-dimensional tables, 4
multi-length arithmetic, xi
multiple-address, **136**, 137
multiple-expression, **123**, 124
multiple-location, 111
multiple-naming, **137**
multiple put, 111, 118
multisets, 28

name, 101, **102**, 105, 106, 107, 125, 129, 135, 136, 137, 141, 142
naming, 103, 104, 109, 117, 121, 122, **137**, 144
negation, 139, 140, **144**
negative constant, 125
new-line, **101**, 107, 109, 120
⸨newline⸩, 64, 69, 72, 75, 86
new-line-proper, 101
new-liners, **111**
⸨next⸩, 78, 82
NO, 12, 70, 144
normalise a polynomial, 42
NOT, 12, 70, 144
not equals, 140
`not.in`, 11, 142
number, 2, 37, 97, 128, 140
numeral, 123, **124**
numerator, 3, 128, 132

operand, 8, 9, 12
optional-*whatever*, **101**
options, 154, 157, 158
OR, 12, 70, 143

164 Index

oracle, 46
order, 5, 97, 140
order-sign, **140**
order-test, 139, **140**
output, 13, 155
output-format, **111**
overloading of functions and predicates, 104, 105, 106
own commands, 72
own functions, 73
own predicates, 74

parameter, 1, 9
paranoid, 58
parentheses, 8, 9, 65, 128
parse, 32
Pascal's triangle, 42
PASS, 114
pass-command, 108, **114**
PATH environment variable, 154
permanent, 103
permanent environment, 88, 103, 108, 109, 112, 115
permanent location, 9, 67, 103, 109
persistence, xi
`pi`, 132
pi, 39, 41
`play`, 87
plus-or-minus, **124**
point, 102
pointers, xi, 31
polynomials, 41
power set, 29
predefined functions, 128
predicate, 74, 104, 105
predicate-how-to, 12, 103, **105**, 109, 116, 117, 141
`previous`, 78, 82
primes, 37
print a list, 26
print an exact number, 38
printable-character, 98, 102, 126

priority of operators, 128
private name, 9, 103, 109, 128
procedure, 8
product of two graphs, 35
product of two polynomials, 42
program, 103
prompt, 63
PUT, 1, 27, 110
put-command, 108, **110**

quantification, 12, 16, 139, 140, **144**
quantifier, **144**
question mark, 63, 154
queues, 29
QUIT, 10, 67, 115
quit-command, 108, **115**, 117, 119
quote, 65, 87, 102, 126

radians, 3
`radius`, 132
`random`, 11, 133
random, 113
ranger, **121**, 144
RAW, 69, 112
READ, 13, 112
read-command, 108, **112**
READ RAW, 69
`record`, 87
recurring fractions, 38
recursive-descent, 32
redisplay, 70
`redo`, 64
refined-command, 108, **119**
refined-expression, 115, 123, **135**
refined-test, 116, 117, 139, **142**
refinement, 13, 70, 75, 106, **107**
refinement-suite, 103, **106**, 107
relation, 33
remainder, 3
REMOVE, 5, 113
remove-command, 108, **113**

Index

removing permanent locations, 67
rename a location, 87
renaming how-to's, 78
REPORT, 68, 116
report-command, 108, 109, **116**, 141, 142
restoring internal files, 156
RETURN, 8, 68, 115
return-command, 108, 109, **115**, 128, 135
reverse order, 43
[right], 78, 84, 86
right-adjusted text, 135
right-test, **139**, 143, 144
root, 3, 131
round, 1, 2, 131
rounding, 2
running ABC, 154, 156
running ABC non interactively, 96

scratchpad copy, 8, 103, 122, 128, 130, 135, 136, 139, 141, 142
screen, 70
SCREEN environment variable, 157
SELECT, 10, 120
select-command, 108, **120**
sentence, 99
sequences, 24
session, 67, 76, 77, 87, 89
SET RANDOM, 11, 113
set-random-command, 108, **113**
sets, 28
SHARE, 9, 48, 68, 109
share-command, 108, **109**
shared name, 103, 109
shift key, 70
side-effects, 24, 103
sieve method, 37
sign, 3, 131
signs, 102
simple-command, **108**, 109
simple-expression, **123**

sin, 132, 133
single-address, 112, **136**, 137
single-alternative, **120**
single-expression, 111, 112, **123**, 124, 127, 128, 129, 138, 140
single-expression-sequence, **111**
single-naming, 105, **137**
SOME, 12, 70, 144
sorting, xi, 5
space between values on output, 17
special tasks, 155
split, 47, 134
square root, 3
stacks, 23
stepwise refinement, 106
string, 3
stripped, 134
strong type checking, xii
strong typing, 90
sub-routine, 8
subtext, 4
SUCCEED, 12, 68, 116
succeed-command, 108, 109, **116**, 141, 142
suggestion, 64, 66, 69, 72, 75
sum of two polynomials, 41
summary of focus operations, 95
suspend, 158
swapping, 1
symbols, 102

table, 6, 15, 97
table, multi-dimensional, 4
table-display, 126, **128**
table entry, 97, 99, 114, 125, 139
table-filler, **128**
table-filler-series, **128**
table item, 125, 126, 139
table-selection, 123, **125**
table-selection-address, 114, 136, **139**
tan, 132
telephone list, 15
template-operand, **105**, 106

template-parameter, **104**
template parameters, 1
template-trailer, **104**
temporary location, 9, 103
TERM environment variable, 154
termcap, 158
terminating-command, **108**, 121
test, 11, 105, 110, 116, 119, 120, 121, **139**
test-refinement, **107**, 109, 116, 117
text, 3, 46, 97, 128
text-body, **126**
text-display, **126**
text-selection, 4
text-selection-address, 114, 136, **138**
tight-expression, **123**, 125
tight-test, **139**, 140, 143
top-down programming, 106
trailer, **117**
train, 7, 9, 11, 97, 121, 128, 141, 144
train-display, 123, **126**
train station simulation, 30
traversing a list in reverse order, 43
trees, xi, 31, 33
type, 110, 139
type-checking, xii, 10, 13

undefined locations, 90
undo, 64, 71, 72, 78, 86
unfilled holes, 77
uninitialised locations, 90
Unix, xiii, 158
unsorted sequences, 24

up, 78, 84
upline, 71
upper, 134
upper-case, 64, 70, 75, 77
user-defined-command, 103, 108, **117**
user-defined-function, 104, 115, 128
user-defined-predicate, 105, 116, 117, 141

value, 1
variable, xi, 103
visit, 76, 77, 89
visit a workspace, 88

WHILE, 121
while-command, 108, **121**
widen, 78, 80
workspace, 88, 89, 103, 155
workspaces, 153
WRITE, 13, 65, 111
write-command, 108, **111**

xterm, 158

zeroadic, 8, 104, 105
zeroadic-examination, **141**
zeroadic-examination-template, **106**
zeroadic-formula, 123, **128**
zeroadic-formula-template, **105**
zeroadic-function, **129**
zeroadic-predicate, **141**

Order form for the ABC implementations

If you can't find ABC on any bulletin board or archive machine that you have access to, you may order a copy using this form, from:
    ABC Implementations
    CWI/AA
    Postbox 4079
    1009 AB Amsterdam
    The Netherlands

For personal computers
Please send me a copy of the ABC implementation:
    For the Atari ST
        ☐ On single-sided disks (360K) ☐ On double-sided disks (720K)
    For the IBM PC and compatibles
        ☐ On 5¼″ disks (360K) ☐ On 3½″ disks (720K)
    For the Apple Macintosh
        ☐ On single-sided disks (400K) ☐ On double-sided disks (800K)

For Unix
Please send me a copy of the Unix sources for the ABC implementation in tar format:
    ☐ On ½″ reel tape
        ☐ 1600 bpi ☐ 800 bpi
        ☐ blocksize 20 ☐ blocksize 1
    ☐ On ¼″ cartridge tape ☐ QIC-24 format ☐ QIC-11 format

Prices
Prices are in Dutch guilders for Europe, and US dollars for the rest of the world. They include all taxes and postage costs, and are correct at the time of going to press.

    On floppy disk: fl. 35 within Europe; $25 elsewhere.
    On reel tape: fl. 100 within Europe; $60 elsewhere.
    On cartridge tape: fl. 250 within Europe; $150 elsewhere.

I enclose a cheque or international money order for .... made payable to "Stichting Mathematisch Centrum, Amsterdam".

    Name: ....

    Address: ....

    ....

    ....

    Country: ....